TOMMY HANDLEY

By

TED KAVANAGH

LONDON
HODDER AND STOUGHTON

FIRST PRINTED . . 1949

*Made and Printed in Great Britain for Hodder & Stoughton, Limited, London,
by Wyman & Sons Limited, London, Reading and Fakenham*

CONTENTS

CONTENTS

ILLUSTRATIONS

" I've brought this for you, sir."
What a card! Tommy with Lind Joyce, Diana
    Morrison and Jean Capra.

THIRD SECTION - - - - *following page* 144

FOURTH SECTION - - - - *following page* 208

CHAPTER I

"THE MAN WHO WAS THURSDAY"

SIX deep they lined the streets; they were of all
ages and of all classes, many were in tears. Slowly
our car nosed its way through the thousands who milled
round the Private Chapel in Westbourne Grove and, at
the other end of the route, ten thousand and more
awaited the arrival of the hearse. Through slum streets,
through squares that had seen better days, on through
more fashionable districts, past blocks of expensive flats,
everywhere it was the same—the crowds had come to
pay a last tribute to one whose voice had cheered them
through the years, to one who had indeed been part of
their very lives. His cheery, " Hello, Folks ! " which
had lightened the gloom of the darkest days had now
become " Good-bye, everyone "—for Tommy Handley at
the height of his popularity, at the peak of his career,
had left the world of laughter which he had created
with a suddenness that had stunned a nation.

Nothing like this had been seen, or experienced,
before, nor was it likely that it would be seen again :
it was a heartfelt tribute to a beloved jester, but it was
also a tribute to the power of the microphone which had
brought his voice into every home in the land, which
had made him a friend of every family, which had raised
him to a position of power and privilege such as no
other comedian had ever enjoyed. There was nothing
hysterical in this national mourning—it was typical of

9

the race to which he belonged; he had made them laugh during a period when laughter was precious, he had stuck to them in all their troubles and, famous and successful though he was, he had always remained one of them.

The car which was taking us to the Crematorium preceded the hearse and thus gave me an opportunity of studying the crowds before that sad moment when all that was mortal of Tommy passed by, when the sense of loss became a reality. I knew that though these many mourners felt that a great part of their lives went with him, so, too, they had taken a great deal of that life which he had spent in their service. I realised that although they regarded Tommy as a personal friend—as indeed he was—few, if any, of them had ever met him. They knew him by his voice alone, and of him it could be said—with absolute sincerity—that the voice was the mirror of the man.

Few, outside his family circle, knew Tommy Handley better than I did, and yet I cannot say I knew him intimately, for he was curiously shy about his personal affairs and extremely reticent about anything concerning his inner feelings. He never wore his heart on his sleeve, and he rarely expressed any particular emotion. In the twenty-five years of our close association I had never seen him lose his temper, nor, in my hearing, had he ever shown the slightest jealousy of his fellow artists—a rare thing in the profession to which he belonged. I am not trying to convey that he was faultless, he was too human for that, but as a Comedian—and he was a great one—he differed greatly from any of his fellows, so many of whom I had worked with and for during all those years.

Since I had first met him in 1925 and had written

one of his first scripts, he had progressed fast and far—far faster and much farther than I had. He had become, without exaggeration, the greatest radio comedian the world had seen, and yet he had not changed. No delusions of grandeur assailed him. Mentally he had grown greatly, principally by reading, by observation and by the constant exercise of his great gifts of comedy. Physically he had not aged as far as appearance went ; he was seldom ill, only on two occasions, to my knowledge, did he miss a broadcast. Yet, during his last years he must have been a desperately sick man. So reticent was he, however, that he never complained, although he suffered latterly from severe headaches and intolerable fatigue. Of course he could have rested, he could have taken life more easily, but he felt his responsibilities so deeply that, ill and worried as he was, he went relentlessly on.

What did this seemingly always cheerful, apparently light-hearted and eminently successful man have to worry about ? He was making a lot of money, he was happily married and wonderfully well looked after by a wife to whom he was devoted, he was firmly entrenched in the hearts of many millions, he was at the top of his profession, his popularity was undimmed, he had no enemies, no near rivals. Radio had afforded him the opportunity of exercising his God-given talent and in B.B.C. circles no one was more popular, more in demand. There may have been many reasons which his reticence prevented him from expressing, but as far as I can penetrate the mask of reserve which he always wore, the primary reason was that in giving so much of himself to others, he had reached a state of mental and physical exhaustion which he was struggling vainly to overcome. Not only on the air had he to be at the top of his form week after week, but he must always be funny in public. It was expected of him—he must not disappoint anyone. His job was the hardest in the world. He could only relax in the privacy of his home, and, as public calls on his services became more and more insistent he saw less and less of the home he loved so much. So conscientious was he that he insisted on answering his fan-mail himself, in his own writing—and he never caught up with it.

No doubt he feared the future—a decline in his power of invention, the inevitable slowing up which age would bring to one to whom speed was so essential. Was his next series to be as successful as the last ? Was he losing his popularity ? And, as one of his oldest friends told me recently, he feared he might grow away from those he knew in less successful days. He feared that his success would estrange those whose friendship he valued. He had become a Great Man, a great public figure, a Royal favourite, an international name, and in his humility he feared it all. That his fears were groundless was proved—alas ! too late—on this, the day of his funeral and, from the vantage point wherein his death had placed him, he must have marvelled as he looked down. " Gosh—this can't all be for me ? " I can imagine him saying. " Personal messages from the Royal Family, thousands of letters from all the corners of the earth, flowers ranging from what they call ' magnificent floral tributes ' down to little anonymous bunches of daffs, crowds at Golders Green and even bigger ones at St. Paul's and at Liverpool Cathedral ? There must be some mistake—I should be rehearsing ITMA to-day."

I was with him the day before he died, for we used to meet in the Savage Club most Saturdays, and this was the only occasion during the week that we could discuss the previous ITMA and chat about the next one. He was in great form, surrounded by his Savage cronies in a corner whence came many a peal of laughter. Less than twenty-four hours later he had the severe cerebral hæmorrhage after which he never regained consciousness. Apparently he had suffered from high blood pressure for some time but, fearing that a doctor would order rest which would prevent him from broadcasting for some time, he did not take medical advice. With the smattering of medical knowledge left over from my student days, I should have recognised the symptoms but they escaped me although I frequently urged Tommy to be vetted, as every man in the fifties should be. No—he felt his responsibilities too much ; he must not let the public down ; he owed a duty to them and to his cast ; he had public appearances to make, Boys' Clubs to open, Charity Matinees, Garden Fêtes, Factories to visit, more Cinema Clubs to appear at, Hospitals to attend, speeches to deliver, Dinners, Lunches, Appeals on and on and on—to St. Paul's Cathedral via Golders Green.

It may seem incredible that such a great public figure as he became should have retained his simplicity, his humility, his kindliness but, in addition of course to his great sense of comedy, it was these qualities which endeared him to his vast radio public. No Scientist has discovered the reason, but it is true to say that the microphone analyses character as no other modern invention can. It has all the penetrative power of the X-ray—it exposes the false and the " phoney," shows up insincerity, debunks pretention and pricks pomposity. In the words of Sir William Haley in a tribute he paid to Tommy in the *Radio Times* : " He had that rare gift which few are born with—and most never acquire—

of being able to broadcast sincerity. As you listened to him you felt . . . the personality of an essentially friendly and good man." And again : " . . . his vitality. He threw himself heart and soul into all he did. The biggest B.B.C. show or the smallest children's party found him ready to give all he had. It was a joy to work with him ; he was so alive, so gay. His shows were always happy ones behind the scenes as well as at the microphone."

I was working on next week's script when I heard of his death, so there was nothing left to do but to turn over the page and to write his obituary for the nine o'clock news. But at once the 'phone rang and continued to ring for hours ; the flat was thronged with reporters, and finally I had to lock myself up in the kitchen to complete it. And I was only one of millions who cried that night. I went to see him lying peacefully in the Chapel, just to say, in his own words, " Ta-ta for now." He had a smile on his face just as I had seen him smile before he cracked a new joke. Our long association had ended, his life was over, a great part of mine had gone. A long time we had spent together with—at least from him—never an unkindly word, never the slightest rift in the lute of friendship and understanding. He had helped me when I most needed it ; any success I had had was largely due to him. I would never meet the like of That Man Again.

CHAPTER II

ILLNESS prevented his widow, Jean, from attending
the funeral. She had returned from hospital only
three days before he died and her doctors forbade her
to leave the flat. So his elder brother, Jack Handley,
his sister-in-law, Francis Worsley (ITMA'S Producer)
and I were Chief Mourners, and indeed we had every
reason to mourn the man with whom we had had so close
an association for so long. Francis lived ITMA, and to
his guidance much of Tommy's continued success had
been due. The sudden exit of the Comedian who had
become so great a part of his daily life and of his B.B.C.
career was a severe blow. So, as we passed slowly
through the dense mass of people gathered at the Crematorium we both realised that with Tommy went a great
deal of what we had built together.

Strange as it may seem, there is something cold about
a crematorium—the ceremony is more impersonal than
a graveyard burial, nor does there seem the same sense
of loss, of finality. The coffin, concealed by banks of
flowers, glides quietly away as the organ plays and all
is over. In addition to the vast crowds, the masses of
wreaths, the many manifestations of grief, the attendance
of so many famous people, this particular ceremony was
distinguished by the beauty of the music. No one who
was there can forget the magnificent singing of Sullivan's
" The Long Day Closes " by Tommy's Brother Savages—

Trefor Jones, Parry Jones, Webster Booth, Walter Midgley, Dennis Noble, Frederick Gregory, George James and Edward Dykes. Here were famous singers saying farewell not only to a famous man but to an old and valued friend, and more inspired singing can seldom have been heard.

This was not to be the end, however, for there was an immediate demand for a National Memorial Service at St. Paul's, and so it was arranged. I was not alone in feeling that after the tremendous " turn-out " on the day of the Cremation, that this would be an anti-climax, but I was wrong. Excellently organised by Clarence Wright—Tommy's partner in most of his public appearances—it proved even more impressive than anything that had gone before. This surely was the first time a Comedian had been so honoured, and not only was the vast Cathedral so full that the doors had to be closed before the ceremony, but so many thousands gathered outside that traffic was diverted and the service relayed to the throng. It was broadcast also to the listening millions. The choir of St. Paul's was augmented by the B.B.C. Singers, conducted by Leslie Woodgate ; the beautiful " Let Us Now Praise Famous Men " was read by John Snagge and the prayer by Dr. Matthews, Dean of St. Paul's. The Bishop of London, the Right Reverend J. W. C. Wand, who was always an ITMA listener, spoke of the Tommy Handley he knew. " He was," he said, " one whose genius transmuted the copper of our common experience into the gold of exquisite foolery. His raillery was without cynicism, and his satire without malice. Who could tell how great a benefit he conferred upon the nation in the days of its grimmest endeavour, as he brought week by week to millions an overflowing measure of irresistible laughter and the

Tommy as a boy

His mother at the age of twenty

John Handley, Tommy's father

The Operatic Baritone complete with wrist watch

R.N.A.S. Concert Party, Roehampton, 1918
Tommy (extreme left) is behind G. H. Elliott, the Chocolate Coloured Coon

The Disorderly Room
(Tommy exposes the ravages of war)

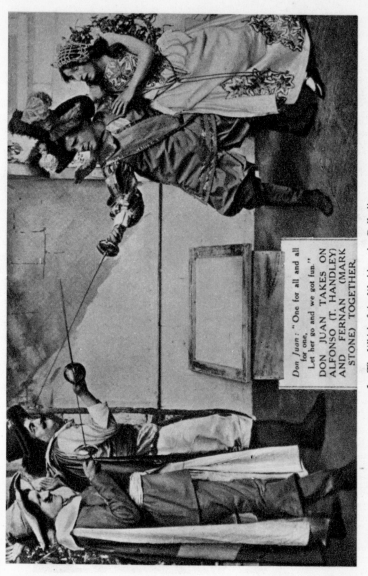

Don Juan: "One for all and all for one,
Let her go and we got fun."
DON JUAN TAKES ON ALFONSO (T. HANDLEY) AND FERNAN (MARK STONE) TOGETHER.

In *The Whirl of the World* at the Palladium

(On left, Mark Stone and Tommy; on right, Nellie Wallace and Billy Merson)

John Sharman and Ernest Longstaffe warn Tommy and company of the dangers that lie in that early example of a microphone

Tommy and Jean at the time of their marriage

Handley and Hylton take a brief rest on the road to fame

John G. Clayton

Tommy when I first met him
in 1926

Tommy as Mr. Winterbottom
(He always loved moustaches)

The two Führers
(Tommy and John Watt, then Director of Variety)

iridescent froth and bubble of the professional jester? From the highest to the lowest in the land people had found in his programme an escape from their troubles and anxieties into a world of whimsical nonsense." The Bishop spoke of the boy who found what he wanted to say about Tommy Handley in his school hymn-book :

> " Teach us delight in simple things
> And mirth that hath no bitter stings " ;

and, he said, even from the phrase, " It's That Man Again," he took away the bitterness that came after a great war. He quoted from a letter sent to him by a Vicar, who wrote : " Tommy Handley came to open a garden fête and gladly agreed to visit the sanatorium, where there was a microphone, so that all could hear his voice, but he refused to use it, and went to every ward with a cheery word for every patient. When I thanked him afterwards, he said : ' Don't thank me, Padre. When you asked me to come I was not particularly anxious to, but, having seen those people, I would have hated myself for the rest of my life if I had not come ! ' "

Again in the Cathedral in Liverpool, Tommy's home town, similar scenes were enacted. The crowds attending the service were said to be the greatest ever known at the Cathedral. Taking as his text—a happily chosen one—" God hath made me to laugh, so that all who hear will laugh with me," the Reverend Eric Evans said : " I speak for many who during the war went down to the sea in ships—I was one of them—and can testify from personal experience to the welcome relief the weekly broadcasts of ITMA brought to us. Tommy Handley was unique in the realm of broadcasting, and he won a place of affection in every rank of society. He was in every sense a true jester."

Thus—once again, no doubt, to Tommy's immense
surprise—did national grief find its outlet. It was, in
fact, international, for the Press throughout the Empire,
the American and Continental papers in addition to
the many pages devoted to his death by our own Press,
all paid their tribute. Letters in their thousands poured
in, for his voice was known far beyond our shores ;
his weekly commentary on events had been listened to
the wide world over—everyone who heard him felt they
knew him, and all felt in their hearts they had lost
something which would never be replaced. In this
connection it may be of interest to quote from a survey
made immediately after his death by " Mass-Observation." In a letter I received from Mr. Leonard England,
he wrote : " I am attaching some of the individual
quotes collected by our investigators and from our
Panel members.

" The analysis indicates overwhelmingly that the immediate reaction to the death of Tommy Handley was
one of shocked incredulity. Everywhere people seemed
to go round telling other people. Some admit to crying.
Many talked immediately of a sense of personal loss.

" A few weeks later the shock and incredulity was
largely gone, although something of this feeling still
lingered. The next reaction was one of missing ITMA
when Thursday came round. The sense of personal
loss of one individual had to some extent spread itself
to regret for the loss of the whole of ITMA, though
most people commented on the fact that everything in
ITMA hinged on Tommy Handley.

" Trying to rationalise or explain their attitudes, some
people argue that the reason for their pleasure in Tommy
Handley was basically that he was the ' ideal ' little
man, facing the problems that they had to face and

succeeding where they failed. But at the same time there was more than this involved, and to most there's also the feeling of having lost a personal friend. Perhaps the impersonal familiarity of the wireless also made a number of people feel that although he was a personal friend he suffered from none of the normal weaknesses of human beings. For instance, one man says : ' I suppose Tommy Handley's voice and personality have become such familiar figures and so sparkling a feature of our lives that we had not considered him to be as frail, fallible or as subject to ordinary physical failings as ourselves.' The feeling of incredulity that he could possibly be dead does, in fact, remain, and more than one person made a remark like this : ' I said to my boy as the funeral passed by : " I bet he's walking round heaven now, saying, ' Hello, Folks ! '."

" Mass-Observation's vast material also includes information on the death of President Roosevelt. To the best of our knowledge, Roosevelt is the only man in the last ten years who has created a similar mass reaction to his death. This is probably partly due to the fact that he also was the epitome of good values who was known mainly through the wireless and whose death was very sudden. But I am sure, as you said, that there is no other comedian who, had he died the same sort of circumstances, would have created the same effect."

Here is a selection of the letters received :

" I still feel very sorry about Tommy Handley's death. I was a regular listener to his Thursday evening programme, and it was a real help to me when I was feeling depressed. Often when I had a bad week at the office, Tommy Handley's quips would brighten my outlook. I miss him very much."—(YOUNG WOMAN.)

" We were sitting listening to the ITMA repeat, when Stuart Hibberd gave out the announcement directly after that Thomas Handley had died. Well, the wife looked at me and I looked at her. It was the way he said *Thomas* Handley—you never heard of him spoken of as Thomas—always Tommy. Well, the wife, she did say : ' It can't be Tommy Handley,' and then Stuart Hibberd said ' of ITMA.' Well, we were stunned—simply stunned. We were very cut up, because he always seemed so natural, as if he wasn't acting from a script. Everyone's sorry."—(WORKING CLASS MAN, aged 50.)

" I did not feel that it could be true after hearing his voice only half an hour earlier. It was as if a friend had left our house and been killed at the end of the street."—(SALESMAN, aged 45.)

" I had just turned the news on casually, as one does, but when I heard the announcement of Tommy's death I did not take in anything else. I was as shocked and incredulous as one is when one hears of the sudden death of a friend. Although I was alone, I sat up in my chair and said, ' Good Lord ' or words to that effect. I had an immediate desire to rush out and tell someone, but could think of no one to tell. So I just sat and got used to the idea, or tried to, but it seemed such a tremendous loss I found it very difficult to believe I would never hear him again with his cheery ' Hello, Folks ! ', or wise-cracking with Frankau."

" I still feel a tremendous sense of loss, as if something that was very much worth having has gone out of life, and life is poorer than it was. There is a big gap on Thursday evenings—not only Tommy himself, but all the other fantastic and fascinating characters with whom he was surrounded and whom we shall never hear again. And I did so want him to get a knighthood—if anyone deserved it he did."—(SECRETARY, aged 30.)

This question of a knighthood was frequently mentioned. He had done a great work for national morale during the war. He was a great favourite with the Royal Family who had honoured him with a Command Performance and had been present at the B.B.C.'s twenty-fifth Birthday celebration at Broadcasting House. Princess Elizabeth, with the Duke of Edinburgh, and Princess Margaret had visited the studio when ITMA was being broadcast. Cabinet Ministers of the three Governments in power from 1939 to 1949 had frequently been present at his broadcasts. He was a great public figure—greater in many ways than many of those who had been honoured, but to my knowledge no approach to him concerning an honour had ever been made. Certainly, he had not been abroad to entertain the troops during the war, but he felt himself—and, indeed, he was advised—that as he was not only doing ITMA for home consumption but " Handley's Half Hour " for World reception, his place was in a Studio where he could entertain and enliven millions day after day instead of isolated groups in far-away places. In this I am sure he was right ; after all, he was primarily a *Radio* man and at the microphone his responsibility lay. He neither wanted nor expected any honour or title— in fact he feared it—it would have meant the end of his career. He could face the public as Tommy Handley—" Sir Thomas " would have meant oblivion to him.

The cast of ITMA returned to the Studio immediately

after the cremation. It was Thursday ; " ITMA Day," but That Man was no longer with us. A script had been prepared, however, consisting of his favourite songs and orchestral arrangements. Members of previous casts—Kay Cavendish, Paula Green and Clarence Wright sang ; the Variety Orchestra played ; John Snagge told the story of a decade of ITMA and paid his own personal tribute to one of his oldest and closest friends. It was a sad show ; it was the end of ITMA ; it was our farewell to That Man.

CHAPTER III

SUCH, then, were the spectacular, unbelievable scenes which were Tommy Handley's farewell to the World he graced so well—a farewell which, accustomed as he was to tremendous popularity, would nevertheless have bewildered and amazed this inherently modest man. It is conventional, perhaps, to suggest here that the great Artist shows irrefutable evidence of his talents almost before he's out of his cradle—the artist is born, not made, and it is certainly true of Tommy that while he was still a very young boy he showed an exuberance of personality and a love for the theatre which must have told all of those who knew him then that, whatever circumstance might decide, fate destined him for a career of bringing entertainment to his fellows.

He was born in Threlfall Street, Liverpool, in 1894, the son of a dairy farmer who died (at the age of 31) while Tommy was still a baby. The result of this bereavement was that Tommy's earliest memories of home were almost entirely of his mother, creating a bond between them which increased as the years passed by. His chief interest as soon as schooldays started was to disguise himself. He spent all his pocket-money on wigs, masks and false moustaches, many of them of the type that were given free with sticks of liquorice and sherbet dabs in those happy, generous days of the early nineteen hundreds. There are many people to-day who recall the horrifying old men who sprang out of bushes and doorways in the days of their childhood as they went down the road to buy a penn'orth of skimmed milk at the dairy. The effect was heightened by the uncanny ability that Tommy had of being able to talk in a man's deep voice. He had indeed a voice of remarkable range. Had he not been a comedian, his future would have been on the Concert platform.

At school, and in the social activities run for the children by the local church, his histrionic exhibitions met with mixed receptions. They did, however, obtain for him a large number of invitations to Christmas and Birthday parties, for young Tom could always be relied on to be the life of those festivities. At least one of these ended in disaster. It was at a time when he had decided to be a ventriloquist. He persuaded all the children at the party, except Johnny Ross, his young host, to leave the room and then he hastily overturned the plants and soil from a window box, shoving the boy inside and placing a large stuffed toy elephant on top. The act, consisting of answers from the elephant to Tommy's questions, went very well until Johnny's father, a sea captain hardened and embittered by long life at the helm in calm and storm, arrived to admire the children at play. Tommy, who well knew that the window box was a particular love of Johnny's father, left the party via the window. The note from Johnny's mother that " the Handley boy need not expect to play with his friend any more " arrived soon afterwards.

Such hitches in the general progress of his career did not upset the budding artist. There were similar mishaps with imitations of chickens laying eggs which not unnaturally broke as they dropped from the clucking Tommy to the carpet of the front parlour in his host's home. His schooldays can best be summed up by his headmaster's comment one day after he had been caught imitating the raucous noise of the old-type cylinder gramophone in class. " Handley," he said, " whenever I hear your name I shall connect it with horrible noises."

It should not be thought, however, that Tommy was a clowning, uncouth boy constantly indulging in exploits typical of Richmal Crompton's " William." The considerable culture which was characteristic of the man in later years when off-duty came largely from his schooling. He was very conscious that his mother was a widow and had something of a struggle. His ambition to better himself so that he could look after her kept him on top of his studies. Reports and conduct sheets which he kept all his life show that he took a lot of trouble with his work. His writing was good (as thousands of listeners who received hand-written notes from him during the ITMA days know), and in history and geography his lively imagination always made up for any defects in knowledge. This stood him in good stead for English composition, and he once won a prize for a competition essay on " The Evils of Strong Drink " which he submitted complete with a drawing of a still.

More successful in forming the foundations of his artistic career was his local branch of the Band of Hope. Every Tuesday evening he went to the church institute run by the Vicar of St. Andrew's. One day the other boys and girls encouraged him to give a rendering of his famous trouser song, which went like this :

> " One day I bought a new dress suit
> To go to a fancy dress ball.
> The waistcoat it was rather large
> And the coat it was too small :

And as for the pants they would not fit,
So I tied them up with string.
And as I waltzed around the room,
I heard the ladies sing . . .
' You're losing 'em ! You're losing 'em !
Hold up your trousers tight.
Whose are they ? Whose are they ? '
Oh, it was a terrible sight."

Miss Cox, the Superintendent, arrived in the outer room and heard the tune of " The Holy City," though the words seemed strange. A mystified Tommy, who had no idea that it was a hymn tune, was led abruptly to the door.

Probably the great entertainment event of the year was the visit to a Liverpool pantomime. As soon as the posters were up on the boards along the streets Tommy began to experience a quickening of the senses —the thrill of anticipation—weeks before the show was due to open. At the back of his rough notebook at school he would make a calendar showing the number of days to go before " The Day " dawned, and every morning he would black out another square. When the great occasion arrived Tommy and his mother would treat themselves to seats in the pit stalls, paying the extra to go in the early doors, and they would sit breathless with excitement watching the rest of the audience come in, reading the programme over and over again until Tommy almost knew it by heart before that never-to-be-forgotten moment when the house lights dimmed.

In his late years Tommy always took his mother to the Liverpool pantomimes, and the Christmas before he died he told me that he had taken her to see the panto which starred the comedian Dave Morris, of whom Tommy was a great admirer. Dave introduced Tommy to the audience, and he stood up to acknowledge the applause. His mother, in her deafness, did not know what it was all about and whispered to Tommy : " Sit down, son—everyone's looking at you ! "

Two features which he especially loved were the chorus singing and the ventriloquist—both of which were included in any pantomime whatever the story might be. He also admired magicians—so much so that for a period he decided to become one, and he spent hours in front of a mirror trying to make cards disappear, or producing coins from thin air. How very real were the thrills of those shows is indicated from the fact that among his effects were programmes from his childhood— and a faded paper flower. It had been thrown by a conjurer and caught by Tommy when he was about nine or ten years of age.

Inevitably, the few weeks of holiday which followed Christmas and the pantomime were occupied with construction of a model theatre based as closely as possible on the one he had visited. Cardboard boxes provided the stage and proscenium ; back drops were hand-painted on paper ; the cast was cut out of cata- logue illustrations. He wrote the plays himself, and his mother was a lonely but appreciative audience. One year the model theatre was constructed on a particularly lavish scale—and Tommy felt justified in issuing invita- tions to his friends and their parents to view a special performance of a pantomime by T. Handley.

His well-known gramophone imitation provided the overture, and then the curtains, made out of an old petticoat, parted to reveal a stage illuminated by a couple of paraffin lamps in the wings. For this im- portant occasion Tommy had permitted his special friend to assist with the dialogue, and they were both surprised and pleased with the reception they got. Every line, even the unfunny ones, was greeted with roars of laughter, but it was not until the audience was almost helpless that the management happened to glance at one another, when they realised that the smoke from the lamps had covered their faces with lamp black as they leaned over the stage.

In summer-time there were holidays in the Isle of Man where some relations lived. There Tommy discovered the next best thing to a pantomime—a pierrot show. It was the Adeler and Sutton company which played in Douglas year after year. Tommy was there three times a day, rain or shine. He got to know the patter, the songs, and the sketches by heart—the entire repertoire. The leading actor of the troupe was 18-stone Charles Harvey, " King of the Pierrots." Naturally Tom did not know it then, but the day was to come when he would play in the same company with that veteran of the boards.

Another artist in the company was J. H. Scotland, the baritone. He had added glamour because he was in lodgings right next to Tommy. When he came home Tommy used to try to attract his attention by singing his songs in a deep voice. One Sunday afternoon, when the vocalist was enjoying a Sabbath rest in his bed-sitting room, Tommy serenaded him with his entire repertoire—" The Bandolero," " The Yeoman's Wedding," and " Asleep in the Deep." Nothing stirred until he roared on a descending note, " Many brave hearts are asleep in the deep, so beware, bee-waare." A weary man leaned out of the window and shouted : " Stop that bloody row." Tommy learned that idols sometimes have feet of clay.

When he was old enough to be allowed to take long

trips by himself, Tommy found a new source of theatrical delight—at New Brighton. On Saturdays he would take the ferry from Liverpool and make his way along the promenade to the theatre. It was a very large place, and its matinee shows had a hard job to entice the public away from the sea and sunshine. It could always rely on one patron even if there was a heat wave— young Tommy. It was at this theatre that he savoured his first real drama. This was W. W. Jacobs' " The Monkey's Paw," with a fine actor of the old school named John Lawson in the lead. The day was particularly fine, and Tommy was the only person in the vast area of the darkened circle. He sat there with his teeth chattering with fright. Afterwards, when he was back in the comforting safety of daylight and people he thought it hadn't been so bad after all, and Lawson became his new hero. In the following week he saw " Humanity," and the week after that a play with the striking title of " A Bride for a Night." Despite its name, the play was thrilling rather than saucy, the climax being a scene where two washerwomen get a man unconscious with drink, tie a noose round his neck, and then wind him up on a gibbet improvised from a rafter and a mangle. To-day, this would hardly seem to be the ideal fare for an impressionable child, but in those robust times there were no committees deciding what people of tender years might or might not view.

The theatre was now thoroughly in his blood. He went to absurd lengths to indicate that he was already closely connected with the stage. His morning walk to school used to take him past the Royal Court Theatre, not far from the Repertory Theatre. In the morning the great doors at the rear of the proscenium would often be open while props were moved in or out, and he found in the general upheaval no one minded much if a small boy wormed his way in and actually stood on the hallowed boards of the stage itself. He used to go early to do this, timing his exit so that some of his school-chums would see him, and—as he hoped—asked him what he was doing there. What he would have said if any of them had shown any interest neither he nor anyone else could have explained. In point of fact, none of them ever saw him. It was one occasion when Tommy's perfect sense of timing went wrong.

In his early 'teens he was in the choir at Toxteth Congregational Church where Tommy's uncle, Mr. Kelly, was the choirmaster. Practices took place on Friday nights, and once again Tommy's mania for enter-taining his friends brought disaster. On this occasion it was a vivid impersonation of his uncle reading the lesson—enjoyed by everyone except the victim of the joke who had come through the vestry door at the crucial moment. Despite this black mark he was invited to take part in the annual church concert—the moment which he had been awaiting. Probably he would have satisfied everyone if he had sung a song, but he was determined to make use of his make-up experience and the monologues he had learned.

Make-up had, indeed, become a fine art by now. His paraphernalia was kept in an old cigar box, and every night he tried a new impersonation before he went to bed, so that often when Mrs. Handley came up to say " Good night " she would find a variety of char-acters in the bedroom. There might be Dr. Fu Manchu, the Chinese menace, with his yellow face, slanting eyes, and long drooping moustache ; or an elderly gentleman of benign countenance, long beard and snow-white hair ; or even the most horrific, knife-slashed, drink-sodden villain out of the Sexton Blake novels he liked to read.

Most of these characters were regretfully rejected as unsuitable for a church concert, and Tommy chose the rôle of an old tramp in the heart-rending sketch entitled "Turn Him Out." To achieve the face of a blue-jowled gentleman of the road on the face of a young boy required plenty of grease paint, and Tommy did not stint it. Unfortunately, he did not finish off with powder with the result that, after polite applause for the act, the paint was starting to run. He did not realise this, and it seemed reasonable that the occasion of his first public appearance deserved wider publicity. Accordingly, he decided to walk home through the streets, just as he was, to let the general public know that there was now an actor in the district. *En route* was an ice-cream parlour. There was a crowd inside and Tommy stalked in and ordered a large cornet. The crowd glanced at him and roared with laughter. Tommy, embarrassed and mystified by this reaction, turned and ran home. A glance in his bedroom mirror told him that drama had indeed become comedy. His face was a mass of red and blue streaks. That was probably the only time that laughter hurt instead of pleased him.

I have already mentioned that Tommy was intensely aware of his widowed mother's circumstances, and her resolute decision that he should remain at school sometimes caused friendly arguments. Tommy felt that he could help the family budget with a few shillings a week if he was allowed to go out to work, as he could have done in those days of easy-going education regulations. One day he thought he had found the perfect compromise. He met a boy who sold programmes at the Empire Music Hall in Liverpool. Fitted out in a neat green uniform with a row of brass buttons, he was able to see the show every night for nothing, as well as earn a shilling or two. It further appeared that the staff was one boy short, and an interview with the wardrobe mistress might prove successful. The good lady, whom Tommy found in the thrilling atmosphere back stage, asked him a few questions, and said he could have the job if he would promise to be there at six sharp every night. There was also the question of a mid-week matinee which would clash with school hours, but Tommy left this particular bridge until the time came to cross it.

It had been as easy as that. On the way home through Sefton Park, one or two courting couples were startled to hear " Program ! Get your program ! " as the budding page practised for his new job.

He rushed into the house to tell his mother.

" I've got a job," he said. " I'm going to sell pro-grems—er, programmes—at the Empire from Monday on."

" You're not," said Mrs. Handley, in that tone which brooked no argument. " You've got homework to do. There'll be plenty of time for jobs when you've left school."

But this set-back on his goal of work in the theatre was possibly not quite so serious as he thought at the time.

CHAPTER IV

HIS SCHOOLDAYS END

THE days before the First World War were wonderful ones for a boy who loved the world of entertainment and all it stood for. The music hall, the theatre, and the concert hall were rich in names whose ability and numbers have never been exceeded. Attracted by the fame which these names brought to entertainment were thousands of idealists, has-beens, never-would-be's and men and women who never gave up hope and ambition even though fortune had passed them by.

The youngsters of to-day who must worship at the shrine of a cinema screen, a distant broadcasting studio, a never-never place called Hollywood, cannot know of the thrills that close contact with flesh-and-blood actors can bring. It didn't matter that these exalted beings were hard put to it to find the price of a night's lodging, that they might have long ago assuaged frustrated genius with the comfort of the bottle, that their repertoire was out-dated even in those tolerant and conservative times—they were actors, a race of men apart.

No doubt there were small boys like Tommy hanging around the Globe Theatre on the off-chance that Master Will Shakespeare might let them walk on in " Henry V " ; they probably hopped around the companies touring the naughty plays by that clever young Mr. Sheridan. One hopes that they will go on haunting the television studios or whatever Mecca there is in the years to come. Of such stuff comes the joy of living.

For Tommy the chance of personal contact with a real actor came just after he left school at fourteen. For one reason or another he did not immediately make for the theatre. One imagines that it was a tussle of wills between his mother, who sighed for signs of her son settling down and losing his childish interests in acting, and Tommy who regarded every day nearer manhood as a step nearer his goal—the Boards.

Opportunity knocked when the local newspaper ran an advertisement : " Competent actors required for Dickensian plays : excellent prospects." Tommy read it and immediately went to the address in an unsalubrious part of the city. He stepped over a child playing in the doorway and knocked. A slatternly woman who opened the door jerked her head in the direction of the stairs. He followed her up flight after flight of the tenement, and was ushered into an attic room. An imposing man, with shaving soap on his face and with a rich baritone voice, invited him in. Tommy was invited to outline his ambitions and experience, the Being nodding sagely at the more interesting details. At the end of the recital he enquired, with an apology for such sordid details, as to whether Tommy had any money. Tom explained that he had saved a few pounds, and this clinched the matter. Mr. Handley could join the company. He was indeed destined to be its financier.

A small hall was booked, and admission was a penny. The first presentation was " Oliver Twist." The Being played Fagin, and Tommy was the Artful Dodger. The Being's wife, a well-nourished woman of some forty-five years, insisted on playing Oliver, which was all right until Bill Sykes had to push her through a window. After several minutes' struggle Oliver was still jammed. Suddenly Bill Sykes had his big idea. He dragged the buxom Oliver from the lintel, and felt dramatically in his trouser pocket.

"Blimey!" he said. "Here's the key. I've had it all the time!"

There were, of course, many shows of this kind in the early years of the century. To-day they seem pathetic. To audiences of those times they were the thrill of their lives. And for a penny, no matter how bad the acting was, the audience got good value for money.

In this particular show the "Being" used to come on the stage between the Acts and do monologues and imitations. Sometimes, if the box office showed more than the usual seven or eight shillingsworth of coppers, he would forget the interlude and go across the road to celebrate success. He would stay there until the pandemonium of the impatient audience reminded him that art and duty called. On one memorable night he forgot that the company was doing "A Christmas Carol," and in its place he provided his patrons with some ghoulish imitations of people having their teeth pulled out. No one seemed to mind very much; they knew "The Christmas Carol" anyway.

At the age of fifteen Tommy went to work with a firm of baby carriage dealers in Duke Street, Liverpool. An old wages book dated 1909 shows that he was paid 8s. 6d. a week at the beginning of his job of office boy. He stayed there until 1917, rising to the position of clerk and salesman. The kindest thing that can be said about his work was that he kept the rest of the staff amused. His own most vivid memories of those days concerned a disgusting liquid with which rubber tyres could be stuck on to pram wheels and also to the toy model prams which sold at a shilling each. The firm encouraged their employees to think up bright ideas to improve trade. Tommy noticed that a fashionable contraption of that time, called a " Baby Walker," ran on extremely stiff wheels. He didn't realise that this was deliberate. Anyway, he went along to the foreman of the workshop and got him to build a " Walker " with ball-bearing wheels. The man looked at Tommy a little queerly, but got on with the job. The model ran beautifully, and the very next day a mother and nurse came in with a fat toddler. The child was placed on the seat and given a gentle push by Salesman Handley. Instantly the child and vehicle shot down the showroom and finished up against the wall. Tommy put on a humorous act to comfort the frightened infant, while his irate mother dragged him out of the straps.

" You're a menace in a shop catering for children," she said. " You ought to be on the stage."

Apart from the adventure with the Dickensian stalwart, probably the first real step he took towards a professional career on the stage was made when Tommy joined a very good amateur dramatic society at Aigburth. It gave shows in St. Anne's Parish Hall, and among the presentations in which he appeared were " Sweet Lavender " and " The Private Secretary." He particularly enjoyed the rôle of Cattermole in the latter play.

The Society had the wealth of humorous adventures and mishaps which seem inevitable with amateurs' efforts. All the members took themselves extremely seriously—including Tommy. He had bought a shilling book entitled " How to Get on the Stage," with the help of which he practised deportment, make-up, elocution, and patter. It even provided diagrams of how and how not to do an act. What more could one desire for a shilling?

Whether or not this technical assistance combined with his natural talent impressed the audience is a matter lost in history, but if enthusiasm could help they must have been good shows. All the spare time of the cast was spent in rehearsals—sometimes a difficult matter because of the mundane necessity of working to earn a living as well.

Stage furniture was borrowed from the mother of the Society's secretary, whose house was fairly near the hall. That lady had little enthusiasm for an arrangement which stripped her front parlour and the best bedroom at intervals, but eventually a compromise was reached that removal would not take place until the last possible minute. Tommy, being a strong young man, was among those who used to make up and put on stage dress before dashing down the road and round the corner to pick up a sofa and couple of arm-chairs five minutes before the curtain was due to go up.

In the best tradition of amateur societies it rarely ascended on time, though the sparse and restive audience had little knowledge of the dramas being enacted backstage. There was the occasion, for instance, on the first night of " Sweet Lavender." The leading lady, known to be in good health and free from temperament, was missing. The girl airily named as her understudy had thought the matter a formality and knew not one word of the part. Threatened with sudden stardom she had hysterics.

The missing actress worked at the local telephone exchange, and it was Tommy who took the obvious step of ringing up the supervisor. He learned that there had been a sudden change in shifts, and the budding Bernhardt was still at the switchboard, too frightened to

mention her imminent duties on the stage. But official-
dom sometimes shows a kindly heart ; the girl was
despatched by taxi, arriving a mere half-hour late.
The delay, of course, caused little comment among an
audience inured to such things.

Among the members of the Aigburth Society was
Frederick Eve. He is now Vicar of St. James's Church,
Ince, Chester. Tommy kept up correspondence with
him, and in the note printed in the issue of the parish
magazine following his death, Mr. Eve commented that
he heard the sad news on the radio on January 9th,
and he believed that the congregation of his little church
must have been one of the first in the country to " remember before the Throne of God His true servant,
Tommy Handley. . . . He was indeed a great and
generous gentleman."

This dramatic society did not provide all the work
that Tommy wanted. He took part in every amateur
entertainment activity that he could find. This was
comparatively simple. With his greed for experience
the matter of fees did not worry him at all, and those
whose onerous task it is to put on good entertainment
without paying for it in aid of the innumerable good
causes supported by such worthy people, soon realised
with some enthusiasm that young Mr. Handley was a
valuable source of income for the funds. War had
broken out, and the number of charity shows in aid
of the forces, comforts funds, and so on, were immense.

Tommy became a member of a concert party which
included names later to become well-known. They
were D. Wise (contralto) ; Jean McMurray (soprano) ;
Fred Hughes (violinist) ; Alf Proffit (tenor) ; B. Williams
(baritone) ; Tommy Handley (comedian) ; and, as
pianist, the lady to whom I am indebted for this

information—(now) Mrs. Jaine Watt. They visited forces' camps, canteens, and hospitals round the Merseyside area, and put on an extremely successful show. Among Tommy's acts was a parody of "The Minstrel Boy" and an act with Alf Proffit called "The Showman." His entertainment never ended with the show—he kept it up all the time on the way there and back, as he did in later years—and occasionally he entertained the company with straight singing at one of the artists' homes. They all tried to persuade him to sing their favourite "Love Could I Only Tell Thee" in the show. He would never do so ; he wanted to be a comedian.

One little historical item which emerges from those days : the party was to give a concert at St. Michael's, Liverpool. Tommy was unable to go, and asked a friend of his to fill the gap. The friend was a little man named Arthur Askey.

In these early war years came still more opportunities —including grand opera ! He was, on the strength of his baritone voice, offered the part of the King in "Maritana." This called for period costume and a beard. Long practice with hirsute adornment of every kind made the latter an easy job, but when the clothes came from the hire company, to his disgust he found that the breeches were festooned with lace. That was too much. No self-respecting King, thought Tommy, could appear before his courtiers in these, and he proceeded to design a regal period costume of his own. This consisted of a pair of high riding boots into which the offending lace could be pushed. From the dashing hat to the swaggering sword scabbard at the waist he looked every inch a Spanish Grandee (though he forgot to remove his wrist watch as proved by a photo still in existence), but from the waist to feet he looked rather like a hard-bitten Westerner out of " Custer's Last Stand." However, it was all experience, and he could justifiably consider himself ready to take the plunge into professional acting if the opportunity arose.

It did—in the summer of 1917. One day in the *Liverpool Echo* he saw an advertisement :

> " A few gentlemen required for musical comedy. Apply stage door, Royal Court Theatre, Liverpool."

During his lunch hour he went straight round to the place he had haunted since he was a small boy, and lined up with half a dozen others. After a while—he was late back to work that day !—a bored-looking gentleman lounging in a chair asked him what he could sing.

" Nirvana," said Tommy.

" What key ? "

" B flat."

With mechanical precision a pianist began strumming the air, and Tommy blundered into :

> " I come from the silent forest,
> My beautiful lotus flower ;
> And I stand in the garden sighing,
> It is the lover's hour."

The piano stopped. Tommy stopped. The man in the corner, still looking bored, grunted : " Leave your address—you might hear something." For six weeks he didn't, and if he had been more experienced and less enthusiastic he might have realised that the words meant virtually nothing. This was, however, the exception.

One morning a postcard came through the letter box :
" Please attend at stage door, Daly's Theatre, London,
at 11 a.m. Monday," it said.

Tommy was cock-a-hoop at the news. His mother
was at first a little doubtful. After thinking things over
she agreed that he should go. She knew that her son
was talking a lot about enlisting, although he had already
volunteered and had been turned down. The Allies'
fortunes of war were at their lowest at that time, and
she privately thought that when the time for uniform
inevitably came it would be something for her son to
feel that he had first tried his hand at the career of his
dreams. And so, on the Sunday night, a young man
set out from Liverpool to the goal he had always had
in mind—London's theatreland.

There were plenty of " chorus gentlemen " round
Daly's stage door when he arrived promptly at 10.55 a.m.,
but the report of the talent scout in Liverpool must have
been better than his bored expression showed, for Tommy
found his engagement almost a formality—at £2 10s. a
week with a touring company of " The Maid of the
Mountains." The chief parts were taken by Tom Shale,
May Beattie and Fred Wright. The company toured
Scotland and the North of England, including Liverpool
—though Tommy's delight at this appearance in his
home town was somewhat tempered by the lowly position
he held in the company. He went to see his friends as
soon as he arrived, and airily told them that he was
understudy to the principal actor—and had to stand in
the wings throughout every show in case that gentleman
suddenly dropped dead on the stage.

The subterfuge was comparatively simple for the first
half of the play because the entire chorus was dressed
as bearded brigands. In the second half Tommy kept

his false moustache on while all the rest were clean-shaven—it is strange the love he had for false moustaches right up to his death—to the delight of the audience and the annoyance of the producer.

Next night he had to reveal himself in his true colours —and that gave the game away. He need not have worried. The fact that their pram shop fellow clerk and friend from the dramatic society was now earning his living on the stage with a London company was enough for his old-time companions. The position didn't matter.

" The Maid of the Mountains " lasted eight weeks. At the end of the run he was offered a job in the next production. He had to refuse—for he had fixed himself up with a much bigger show than any being organised in the offices around Leicester Square and Shaftesbury Avenue. Tommy had at last been accepted for the Royal Naval Air Service.

CHAPTER V

THE R.N.A.S. AND AFTER

TOMMY became a member of His Majesty's Forces on November 11th, 1917—just a year before the Armistice. He was posted to the kite balloon section, with his unit stationed at the Crystal Palace, Sydenham. After the usual routine of " square bashing " and discipline, he was sent aloft in a new type of observation balloon to be used for artillery spotting. The thing did not rise quickly enough, and the officer in charge ordered a rather frightened AM2 Handley to throw out some of the sand ballast. The enthusiastic rookie, anxious to obey orders promptly, heaved a complete sack overboard. The balloon was little more than a hundred feet up at the time, and he just had time to see the numerous brass hats and experts who were watching the test dodge for cover as he was carried aloft at the rate of an express lift until the hawser jerked the crew almost out of the basket.

Later came some tours of duty at Sheerness on patrol boats, and then he was posted to Roehampton. The boring routine of service in the back areas did not make any more appeal to him than to anyone else. After three years of war the authorities were at last becoming alive to the importance of morale—and the help that good entertainment for men out of the actual fighting line could provide. All units were told to search out men with ability to entertain, and Tom naturally put in his

43

name. The idea of a comic did not appeal to the officer-in-charge (probably he had learned of the skits that enthusiastic rankers put on under the safety of grease paint and protected by the footlights), and Tommy had to be satisfied with a classification of " singer, baritone, light songs, of."

He was thereafter in great demand at concerts where, in spite of his efforts to be a baritone, he found the audience always laughed, even when he got to the usual third verse in the minor key. Then one night the elocutionist, who boomed out patriotic poems, was taken ill. No substitute could be found, and so they asked Tommy if he would take his place. With his usual enthusiasm he agreed, and decided mentally that he would give a rendering of that dramatic monologue of Empire-builders, " The Green Eye of the Little Yellow God " which he thought he knew backwards. He started off in a dim light with a vibrating deep voice :

> " There's a little yellow idol to the north of Khatmandu,
> There's a little marble cross below the town,
> There's a broken-hearted woman . . ."

By this time the audience was convulsed with laughter, and Tommy, thinking he might as well make the best of a bad job, gave up and went into his own version of that well-known piece. From then onwards he became officially a Comic. He was not allowed to give up his singing entirely, and in consequence he joined the station's choral society, who were giving performances every few months. Tommy had been keen on D'Oyly Carte company shows, and had been rehearsing some of their operas with the operatic society at home when he got his London job. He knew several of the Henry

Lytton songs. It is not surprising therefore that he was cast to play these parts in the camp productions. Amateurs' genius for hilarious accidents did not desert this company. In a performance of " The Gondoliers " the gondola containing the Duke of Plazo-Toro, his wife and daughter sailed in a second or so too soon, leaving the Duke seated off-stage on a piece of wooden prop so that he had to make his entrance apparently wading knee deep in the canal after his wife and daughter had disembarked. The authorities gave up the ideas of culture after that, and decided that comedy, when deliberate, was best.

A concert party was formed. The members of it became privileged persons—excused almost all duties, and as these consisted principally of rolling the camp's cricket pitch the war effort did not suffer. After giving one or two shows around Christmas, 1917, the party was allocated official status. Gus McNaughton managed and produced the shows. The other members of the party were C. B. Stevenson, Pat O'Connor, Joe Mott, Jack Kelly (professionally known as Jackson Owen), G. H. Elliott (The Chocolate Coloured Coon), Reg Vickers, and Miss Durden. They were kept very busy, giving an average of three shows an evening in the London area. On several occasions they gave a performance on the plinth of Nelson's column. At that time Trafalgar Square was transformed into a model of a ruined French village. The towering height of the Column, the ruined village which surrounded its base, and the searchlights playing on a small group of people singing music hall songs, produced a curiously macabre effect. But perhaps the strangest stage Tommy ever played on then or afterwards was the top of a tank. Recruiting parties used to travel round the streets in tanks, stopping every few hundred yards to collect a crowd. Someone in the War Office had the bright idea that the top would make an excellent stage for a performance by the concert party, and although it was uncomfortable the show was very well received.

The high-light of the party's career was the occasion on which they were all presented to Princess Louise. This was a concert given at the Chiswick Empire on January 22nd, 1918, in aid of Queen Mary's hospital for limbless servicemen, now the famous " Star and Garter " homes. After the show the Princess congratulated Tommy and the rest of the cast on their performance—the first of several Royal presentations he was to have in his subsequent career. All that spring and summer the concert party continued its good work, and then with autumn came the signs of victory. Tommy celebrated Armistice Night with the millions in London. Soon there was demobilisation and a need to pick up the threads of a career which had barely begun little more than a year before.

Those twelve months in uniform had been a wonderful investment of experience for Tommy Handley. The young man who started to go round the agents along with thousands of others anxious to get " back to normal " was no longer a rather wide-eyed lad from Liverpool, thrilled at any job which would get him on the stage. He had learned more about holding an audience in those war-time shows than he could possibly have done in five years of peace-time tours. Three shows almost every day to tough service audiences, munition workers, and the like, would make or break any performer. Add to that the job of unadulterated busking in the War Loan and recruiting drives, given at street corners in competition with the roar of the traffic with every type of audience from dockers in Limehouse to stockbrokers outside the Royal Exchange, and you have a routine which would appal anyone who had not been born for the job.

During its twelve months' career the concert party gave something approaching a thousand shows, and for Tommy, at least, it meant some different patter every time. It demanded an ability to fight the audience for its attention and approval ; and it developed his flair for swift, good-humoured repartee.

All this experience did not mean that he was to find success just around the corner. The switch-round from war to peace did not run as smoothly as in the nineteen-forties. There were hundreds of men for every job, and the queues of applicants for " shops " on the stage were just as long as everywhere else. He was lucky enough to have a friend from his R.N.A.S. days who tipped him off about a touring company being formed to take a musical comedy called " Shanghai " on a short provincial tour. It was a MacDonald and Young show, and Tommy got a chorus part with a few lines of dialogue in some of the many scenes. On the way back to his lodgings he met a friend from Liverpool who was on his way to an audition of a very different kind—that of a singer in the chorus of the D'Oyly Carte's operatic company at the Savoy. Tommy said he would walk part of the way with his friend to pass the time. Eventually he got talking and decided to step inside to listen. His friend knew that Tommy had always been a keen Gilbert and Sullivan fan and that he had played in several of the operas in an amateur capacity. He suggested that for the fun of the thing Tommy should ask for an audition himself. When the manager called out " Next ! " Tommy stepped on the stage.

" Will you kindly play the Major-General's song from ' The Pirates of Penzance '," he asked the pianist, secretly amused at the way jaws were dropping amongst the auditionees all over the theatre. The reason was that this is a quick-fire song, and a most unlikely one for a newcomer to suggest for a try-out. But Tommy, who loved very fast talking, knew the song well. He had played the part in the amateur operatic society in Liverpool before the war, and he sang it in great style. At the end of the song he was astonished to hear a voice from the stalls saying : " Do you know any more of the Gilbert and Sullivan numbers ? "

" Yes, sir," said Tommy. " I know most of them."

" Right ! Let's hear ' Tit Willow '," replied the voice, and the pianist promptly played the opening bars.

Tommy sang it as best he could, and after the usual " Thank you " prepared to go home. He was told to leave his name and address, but by this time he knew that such a request meant little—if anything.

Later that week he set out on his tour with " Shanghai," and it was not until some weeks afterwards that, on a visit to London one week-end, he was told by his land-lady that a representative from D'Oyly Carte had been continually ringing up. Out of interest he went round to the Savoy, where he was told that if he was free right away he could join the No. 2 Gilbert and Sullivan Company.

He had to explain that he was already signed up with the " Shanghai " company, and so the chance of becoming a Savoyard was lost. It is strange to ponder on the different career he would have had if that audition had been just a few days earlier.

But " Shanghai " was quite good fun. One of the scenes in which Tommy had a speaking part concerned a pirate junk, in which he played the rôle of the captain, complete with long drooping moustaches and a pigtail.

The first night that the company played at Cambridge the undergraduates yelled to Tommy : " Take off that moustache ! " He ignored them for a while, for like most shows of its type, the accent was on music more than comedy. But they kept on shouting " Take it off," and as he had a lively knowledge of the capabilities of thwarted students in wrecking a theatre, he thought he'd better humour them. He dragged off the left half, and just as he was going to take off the other piece, the audience shouted " Leave it on ! Leave it on ! " He played the rest of the show with only half a moustache, and Tommy the pirate was the success of the evening. Whenever he went off stage after that they groaned mournfully, " He's glone, he's glone ! " The leading players were not exactly pleased with the chorus gentleman who had stolen most of the limelight and turned the show into something bordering on slapstick.

The musical director of that show was Jack Hylton, down in the " Shanghai " programmes as Jackson Hylton. It was the start of a friendship which was to last for a lifetime, and later on Tommy was destined to tour under the Hylton banner.

" Shanghai " folded up in the late spring of 1919. Jack Hylton was detailed to form a concert party to cover the summer season at Bognor (not then honoured with the suffix " Regis "). It was a very popular resort, and the very good cast sent down included Charley Harvey, " King of the Pierrots," previously mentioned as an idol of Tommy from the days in the Isle of Man. During the war Charley had steadily climbed the popularity ladder, and was by then the premier concert party comedian of the country, with a number of seasons at Blackpool to his credit. It can be realised that when Tommy was given the rôle of second comedian there must have been a lot of people impressed with his ability —especially as he was still unknown to the public, certainly in the South. There was, as a matter of fact, some argument about the wisdom of the choice, but the enthusiasm of Jack Hylton who had watched Tommy from the conductor's rostrum night after night on the " Shanghai " tour, finally prevailed on the management to take a chance.

As it turned out, Tommy proved a good insurance policy for the promoters. Charley Harvey did not quite repeat his success up North. This was at least partly due to the competition he received from Tommy, who seized every opportunity that the day's news and the audience out front offered in order to make a topical gag. He was developing something quite new to artistes of the old school—spontaneous patter.

Charley had a very different style. Some might call it the Bludgeon Technique. There was the wet afternoon, for instance, when he sang, to an apathetic handful huddling in the deck chairs from a howling wind, his favourite song :

> " One day I was taking a walk down the street,
> I saw a small boy with no boots to his feet ;
> It did look so sad to see him standing there,
> So I went to a fruit shop and bought him a pair."

Down in the deck chairs no one stirred. Charley turned round to Jack Hylton at the piano and said : " We'll try it again, Jack." He sang the last line again. Still no one laughed. Charley fixed his gaze on an old lady in the front row, leaned down and boomed :

" I've just sung a very funny joke, madam. You're supposed to laugh at it, madam. And now we'll have it again, madam. This time I want to hear you laugh, madam." Of course, it worked. The entire audience—all twenty of them—tittered. Afterwards Charley said to Tommy : " Here's a good tip, my boy. If you can't make 'em laugh, frighten 'em." It is one piece of advice from an old trouper that Tommy never took.

Tommy's personal triumph at Bognor resulted in Jack Hylton suggesting to Tommy that they should join forces as a double act. Tommy agreed, and they had a try-out at the famous old Bedford Music Hall, Camden Town, in October, 1919. It went over as well as anything ever did with the most critical audience in the world—the Cockney in the gallery.

Next move was a little higher in the social scale—to Lyons Popular Café in Piccadilly, now a B.B.C. Studio. It was a good booking—£30 a week, and the prospect of subsequent engagements right round the hotels and restaurants owned by the company. But high hopes were dashed. The diners at this very large restaurant wanted little more than background music with their meals. Jack and Tommy did their best, but they couldn't make themselves heard above the general pandemonium ; and, of course, this was before the days of microphones and amplifiers.

The subsequent bookings which had been half-promised did not mature—and several rosy prospects which hinged on the success of the Café contract didn't come off either. One typical heartbreak was when an agent approached them in Charing Cross Road and asked if anyone was handling their business affairs. The somewhat disconsolate pair, who had little beyond the £30 paid the week before, said " No."

" Let me look after you. I like your act. I'll come
round on Monday."

This sounded like opportunity knocking, and so Jack
and Tommy invested in a half-bottle of whisky to give
the agent something in which to celebrate the new tie-up.

" If we open the bottle in front of him," Jack observed,
" then he'll think we're not drinkers, and we've bought
it specially for him."

As neither of them aspired to the luxury of a taste
for whisky, Tommy solved the problem by pouring a
couple of doubles down the sink. The agent duly
arrived, and sat chatting to them until he had drunk
all the whisky. Then he told them how he was going
to book Johnny Fuller, a pantomime cat act, for a big
Christmas show. With that he got up, shook them both
effusively by the hand, and said, " Good night, boys.
I must see your act some time."

But Tommy's lucky streak still held. He " rested "
for a week or so, and then a burlesque written for the
vaudeville stage by Con West, entitled " Seasoned to
Taste," with music by Jack Hylton, was due for casting.
There were six in the act. Tommy was the comedian,
a young man named Bobby Howes was given the rôle
of second comedian, and Dorothy Frostick was the star.
The act opened at the Metropolitan, Edgware Road,
on December 1st, 1919, and although Tommy and
Bobby made personal hits, the show as a whole was not
well received. The curtain went up to show a big cruet
on the stage, with four people to represent the condi-
ments. Bobby Howes was pepper, Tommy was a waiter
who got the biggest laugh in the show by looking darkly
into the wings and saying, " I don't know what you
mean by a soldier's farewell." He also did a comic
dance in a ballet skirt.

He had a wealth of amusing anecdotes to tell of this show's chequered career. There was the time, for example, when Bobby Howes could not make the first night of the engagement at the Hulme Hippodrome. The booking had been made on the understanding that he was in the show, and the bills all announced the fact. The stand-in, named Jack Frost, was tipped off to say he was Bobby if any questions were asked.

It was one of those nights with a hoodoo on it. "Vinegar" didn't turn up either. The empty bottle in which he was supposed to stand fell over with a crash and rolled into the footlights. Everyone fluffed their lines. When they crept off the stage the manager was waiting for them. He said to Jack : "Who are you ? "

" Jack—er—Howes."

Tommy hastily came to the rescue. "He means he's Bobby Frost."

" Well," said the manager, " it doesn't really matter ; for the rest of the week your act is cut from thirty minutes to ten."

" Seasoned to Taste " struggled on well into 1920, and when it finally died a somewhat belated death Jack Hylton approached Herbert Clayton, partner in the agency of Norris and Clayton, with a proposition that both Tommy Handley and Bobby Howes should be put under contract for three years, with the right to sublet them to other Managements. It guaranteed them both a minimum of forty weeks a year. Tommy could justifiably write to his mother, as he did with more-than-weekly regularity, to tell her that he was now firmly on the ladder.

This contract meant a tremendous variety of work and wonderful experience. The first " shop " was for

a concert party at Llandrindod Wells. This was a
production of the Walls and Heighley partnership, later
to be known as Walls and Henson.

It is somewhat difficult to imagine the bland comedian
Leslie Henson in a rage, but one of Tommy's favourite
stories about the show at Llandrindod Wells concerned
the second night of the season. The contralto was
singing " Down in the Forest." Just as she reached
her top note a little man who was sitting in the front
row of the stalls rose from his place and walked slowly out
—on tip toe. He was wearing very squeaky boots, and
the whole theatre could hear him. Henson was furious,
and as soon as the song was ended he caught the little
man in the entrance hall.

" What the devil do you mean, sir," he spluttered,
" by coming here with the deliberate intention of ruining
our performance a few minutes after it has started.
Your behaviour is disgusting." He let the man know
what he thought about him until he ran out of breath.

The offender had looked more and more crestfallen as
the tirade went on. In the pause he said : " I'm terribly
sorry, sir. You see, I happened to look at my watch,
and I realised I've been keeping my wife waiting for
three minutes. I must fly now, or . . ."

To Tommy, who had been watching the incident,
not the least amusing part was the amazing change
which came over Leslie Henson's face. A second before
he had been in a towering rage, but when he heard
the absurd excuse, all the anger faded from his face
in an instant, and he burst into roars of laughter.

More personal anecdotes include the time when the
Heavy Man was suddenly taken ill with appendicitis.
Tommy was asked to play the part at a moment's
notice. The minor point that he did not know the lines

did not worry him. He carefully wrote them on pieces of paper and pinned them up in various parts of the stage set according to the place where he would be at that stage of the dialogue. His opening lines were inside his bowler hat, and his " dying words," made while he lay shot on the stage, were concealed in the footlights. No one in the audience knew that the villain hiding behind the big black moustache was prancing from one verbal life-saver to another until blessed relief came in the shape of a bullet from the heroine's gun. She saved her virtue and Tommy saved his reputation for never running dry on the stage.

With his well-known versatility it is not surprising to learn that when the " Light " man was unable to appear it was once again Tommy who filled the breach. The act was the singing of a chorus number while the rest of the company stood in a semi-circle marking time. Tommy knew the words of the chorus all right, as did everybody else, but he was not at all sure of the verses which he had to sing solo. He managed the first few lines and then marched round the semi-circle tapping each with his stick and singing " Don't know it ! Don't know it ! Don't know it, I don't ! " The words fitted the music well, the band played a little louder, and the audience had no idea that anything was wrong and applauded vigorously at the end.

CHAPTER VI

FROM FIT-UPS TO A ROYAL COMMAND
PERFORMANCE

AFTER the North Wales booking came all kinds of engagements, including a period in a revue called " Lightning," produced by Jack Waller. Tommy still wanted all the experience he could get—in as wide a variety of entertainment as he could find.

He must have had all—and more—than he wanted when he was for a period with a " fit-up " show. The younger generation which has radio and television on tap, and a cinema down the road, or at least on a 'bus route, will not know of the thrill that the news " a fit-up's coming next week ! " brought to everyone from the Squire to the village idiot in the rural England of thirty and more years ago. At the time Tommy joined one, this grand old form of travelling entertainment was fighting a losing battle against the silent cinema, though in a more stream-lined version it had a big revival during the last war, when ENSA found that lonely camps got a bigger kick out of a small live show than any mammoth Hollywood all dancing all colour all starring musical. It's a pity that the lesson has so soon been forgotten.

Anyway, it will be obvious that a fit-up show was a portable theatre made in bits and pieces which could be fitted to almost any sized barn, village hall, church annexe, or schoolroom. It is probably the oldest form of theatrical show in Britain—as old as the ancient fairs from which it presumably came.

In the period after the First World War prices charged were generally 1s., 6d., and 3d.—with " standing room 1d." if things were very bad.

A typical time-table, kept by Tommy, covered an ordinary week.

Sunday.—Strike fit-up, and get scenery and everything ready for packing on to lorry. Afternoon : Rehearse in bare hall the Monday show.

Monday.—6 a.m. : Up, and down to the hall. Pack fit-up, scenery, props, and so on into the lorry ; climb aboard and start off. The lorry drops the cast at the nearest station and goes on with the equipment by itself. There is a three-mile walk from the station to the new " stand." Afternoon : All hands work frenziedly to get the fit-up rigged in time for the evening show. 7 p.m. : Knock off for rest. 7.45 p.m. : Early doors (2d. extra) open. One of the cast takes the money ; another acts as usher. 8.15 p.m. : Curtain rises on " Lady Audley's Secret "—or " The Well of Death." The show is over by 10.45 p.m.—but there is no rest yet. Two shows are to be given on the following day, and the actor-manager calls for a quick read-through before bedtime.

Tuesday.—First call 7 a.m. for a rehearsal of the matinee show. Breakfast afterwards at 9 a.m. Down to the hall to prepare the stage for the matinee. 11.30 a.m. : Dismissed to read up part in evening show. 1 p.m. : Midday meal. 1.30 p.m. : Dress rehearsal of matinee. 2.30 p.m. : Doors open. 3 p.m. : Curtain up. 5.15 p.m. : Matinee over ; all hands set stage for evening show. 6 p.m. : Tea. 6.30 p.m. : Repeat of previous evening.

Wednesday.—First call : 10.30 a.m. for rehearsal for

evening show. 12.30 p.m. : All go out distributing handbills and canvassing for evening audience. 2 p.m. : Midday meal. 3 p.m. : Rehearsal. 5 p.m. : Rest until 7 p.m., then as other days, except that afterwards everything must be packed in readiness for the next move.

Thursday, *Friday* and *Saturday* were repeats of the earlier part of the week, except that an extra show is given on Saturday morning for the children.

This was a routine week in rural areas. Occasionally the theatre would arrive at a market town, and the stand might last as long as a fortnight. That meant twenty shows—eight matinees and twelve evening performances—and of these, at least sixteen were different shows. Actors and actresses doubled two or three times in each play, so they had at least thirty-two parts to learn.

Tommy loved this work and believed that the experience was the best he ever had. It might be thought that melodrama would not be the sort of work he wanted. Actually the audience got more than drama. Between the acts members of the company gave variety turns while the others changed the scenery. At the conclusion of the main play there were more variety turns while the stage was set for a " Screaming Farce in One Act." It wasn't bad value for 6d., and many people will agree with the view Tommy held that it could compete with the cinema even to-day.

Needless to say Tommy became very popular in the variety section. He could try out all sorts of gags, lines of comedy, and patter to his heart's content. The proprietor of the fit-up show was an old-stager. He had been born in a portable theatre, had played Little Willie in " East Lynne " at the age of four, and had been on the road ever since. The cast called him the Guv'nor. He regarded them as his children, and loved them like a father.

The season eventually came to an end, and in the time-honoured manner the Guv'nor said that the final night was to be for the benefit of the cast. The show was given at Henfield, Sussex, and everyone agreed that they should celebrate by spending their " take " on a week-end at Brighton. Unfortunately no one had troubled to tell them that the local squire's son was coming of age on the same day, and the villagers were being treated to a general celebration up at the Hall, complete with fireworks, cakes, and ale. The company shared out that night's takings in the ratio of 1s. 4½d. each. The Brighton trip was off—and Tommy headed for London.

Walls and Heighley had some news for him. Leslie Henson had dug out a sketch which had amused the troops in France. He thought that war weariness had passed sufficiently to try it on civilian audiences. Tommy was given the script to read. The author was Eric Blore, destined to become famous for his obsequious butler rôles in Hollywood films after talkies came, and the main feature was that all the dialogue was set to popular music. Tommy was (one of the rare occasions that his judgment of public tastes was in error) unimpressed with the idea. As he was, however, under contract his protest was largely formal, and he soon found that whatever he might think of the sketch, the public loved it.

Its name was " The Disorderly Room."

There is no possible way of estimating the number of times Tommy played the officer in charge in that riotously funny skit of army procedure. It started to

go the rounds of the Halls in 1921. At first the bookings
were occasional. Soon they became more and more
numerous, until it looked as if Tommy would be known
by that sketch alone. Wisely he did not ignore other
jobs, and " The Disorderly Room " became a sort of
a standby in his repertoire. He played it on and off
from 1921 to 1941. It must have been played on every
music hall stage in the country. I myself saw it on a
medical student's night out in Edinburgh. With such
a wide audience it naturally brought national fame to
Tommy, and for the first time he became a name among
tens of thousands of the public. The first time his name
appeared in lights was as the star of " The Disorderly
Room." It was playing at the London Coliseum. He was
not unnaturally very proud to see the sign and resolved
to have a photograph taken of it to send to his mother.

He went to see a photographer about it who agreed
that he could manage it on Saturday night—the last
night of the show. But Saturday's twilight came in
with a real old " London particular," and that memorable occasion never got registered on celluloid.

That was at a later date when the sketch had reached
West End standards. Its beginning was at the Shep-
herds Bush Empire with six in the act. Later Tommy
reduced it to five people.

The charm of " The Disorderly Room " was undoubtedly the way the words were fitted on to popular
songs of the moment. In the original version it opened
up with a soldier giving evidence against the prisoner
to the tune of " They Called it Dixieland " :

> " He took a tin of sardines and some clothes,
>   And he pinched my dixie, too ;
> He took a piece of cheese and po-ta-toes,
>   What was in my dixie too.

> He pinched the only socks I got.
> Yes, he pinched the blooming lot.
> Nothing was forgotten
> From a penny reel of cotton
> To some polish in a penny pot."

During this piece of evidence Tommy, as the officer in charge, used to pick up a ruler and start pointing to the exhibits as they were mentioned, making a considerable clatter in the process. It all sounds rather foolish, but there were signs of that crazy exploitation of every possible pun, of cartoon drawing in sound, that made Tommy Handley the perfect broadcaster. "The Disorderly Room" was not really a visual show, though its producers at the time probably did not think of this. It had originally been written as a sketch which could be performed with a minimum of props in a minimum of space in make-shift halls in France. It depended on its laughs for its musical skits, bad puns, and the de-bunking of military red tape. Tommy's own opening speech to the prisoner was purely aural humour. In a parody of a current George Robey hit, he sang :

> " It appears you waxed excessively convivial,
> With fine fermented produce you had strife.
> You gazed upon the vintage when 'twas crimson,
> When Bacchanalian revelry was rife.
> You've partaken of thoracic lubrication,
> With ambrosial nectar you were somewhat lined.
> It clearly states you were *non compos mentis*,
> In other words . . . "

Here the Sergeant-Major used to cut in with " You was blind ! "

Now it is doubtful whether one per cent. of the audience had ever heard or could understand the

majority of the words in that lyric until the Sergeant-
Major gave his helpful elucidation. Nevertheless,
Tommy was showing his indefinable ability to talk
Greek to the English and make himself understood.

Often he used to experiment with sheer gibberish.
He would change after the fourth line into :

> " You've partaken of the tittifolol bazooka,
>   With the Skimsons and the Skamsons on your mind.
>   When the Cleethorpes are magoozlum in the zimzam,
>   In other words . . ."

Here was a slight indication of the shape of words
to come.

It is small wonder that " The Disorderly Room "
went on and on. It was recorded, filmed, broadcast,
and eventually televised. It became so well-known with
some music hall audiences that they were able to shout
the lyrics in unison with the cast.

It was given the final hall mark of fame when it was
included in the Royal Command Variety Show at the
Coliseum in 1924. But probably an even more significant sign of its popularity, as well as the way the name
of Tommy Handley was connected with it, is the fact
that letters were accepted and forwarded by the Post
Office though they bore just the words : " Officer-in-
Charge, The Disorderly Room." An even more bizarre
effort which came through all right was addressed :
" Tommy Handley, c/o The Disorderly House."

There was something unique about " The Disorderly
Room " sketch which could not be imitated. In the
latter half of 1922 Tommy worked occasionally in a
skit which was basically a civil court version of the
court martial idea. It was called " Wrangle v. Wrangle,"
and was set entirely in the Divorce Court, with all the
words to music of popular tunes. There were some

extremely bright ideas in it from the word " Go." The barristers entered to the music of " Lustige Bruder," doffing white gloves in the manner of Albert Whelan's classic entry for his act, and the verbal duel between Mr. Wrangle (Tommy) and his mother-in-law went to the tune of " Colonel Bogey."

Kathleen Keating, the other Wrangle (the wronged wife), entered to the Pizzicato from " Sylvia," and subsequently warbled dolefully about her married life, " Every morn he shows me violence."

With the reputation of Tommy in " The Disorderly Room " plus the fact that the sketch was written to the same formula, encouraged the booking managers to give it a run. It played the Coliseum, the old Alhambra, and the Holborn Empire, as well as the key provincial halls. But it just didn't click, and after six months the idea was abandoned. Possibly at that time divorce was not regarded as a humorous subject ; or the public wanted the original, not a substitute. Anyone who can gauge public taste by saying why one show should be a phenomenal success and the other a failure would make a fortune in the entertainment world.

Despite the blight of failure, the Wrangle v. Wrangle company had a very happy time on tour. It was the height of the " Beaver ! " craze when the Bright Young Things of the twenties—as well as lots of people young enough and old enough to know better—toured the streets to shout " Beaver ! " at old men with beards. Good as this recreation was for the high spirited, Tommy added further piquancies by a scoring list based on the the rarity of the Beaver halloa-ed. Top marks (never scored by any of the competitors despite the most assiduous search) were for a red beaver on a mauve bicycle.

The winter of 1923-24 is notable for the fact that Tommy appeared in a pantomime—" Dick Whittington "—his one and only pantomime, followed by a revue at the Palladium, " The Whirl of the World." The cast included Nellie Wallace, Billy Merson, Ethel Hook —Dame Clara Butt's sister—and Nervo and Knox. After a time Billy Merson left to take a part in the first production of " Rose Marie," and Charlie Austin came to take his place. This was the beginning of the era of lavish musicals. Cochran, De Courville, Charlot— were spending thousands in dressing their shows with a magnificence which has not been excelled before or since.

It was in a scene with Nellie Wallace in " The Whirl of the World " that Tommy made an unconscious *faux pas*. There was a burlesque of the balcony scene from " Romeo and Juliet," played by Billy Merson and Nellie Wallace. Before Romeo actually appeared, several other men, dressed as troubadours, had to walk into the garden and gaze soulfully at Juliet's window. Tommy was one of them. One night, however, he was duly strolling across the stage when he became aware that the stage manager was signalling him violently from the wings. Tommy sauntered off as nonchalantly as possible, to be told in an urgent whisper that Billy Merson had been taken suddenly ill and someone must take his part in the burlesque. That someone was to be Handley. He determined to rise to the occasion.

The routine was that Billy Merson came on, playing a ukelele. Nobody came on the balcony, and so he threw a brick through the window, whereupon out popped the head of the gentle Nellie Wallace, who cried " Who the hell threw that brick ? " It finished with Merson climbing up a rope ladder to get on the balcony.

This seemed fairly simple to Tommy, and he got as far as throwing the brick. Nothing happened, but he could hardly have known that Nellie Wallace was having a back-stage discussion about methods to cut the sketch to save Tommy from too much of an unfamiliar routine. He decided that he would have to keep the scene going as best he could, and started to climb the rope ladder. The climb was none too easy without practice, as most people who have tried a rope ladder will know. The audience took it all as part of the act and roared their approval of the funny man performing monkey-like acrobatics in mid-air, getting his legs caught up between the rungs, and having the utmost difficulty in disentangling them. Spurred on by the laughter, Tommy at last found himself on the balcony, but there was still no sign of Juliet.

Realising he would have to say something, Romeo suddenly had a brainwave. Turning to the audience with an engaging smile, he took them into his confidence by saying, " Where is Juliet ? " There was a pause while he looked in at the window. " Ah, I see her now—she's emptying the pots and pans ! "

The audience yelled with delight, with certain exceptions where grim-faced ladies sat with poker faces. Then Tommy realised that a remark which would have been most appropriate for a ground floor kitchen window, was hardly right for a commentary on Juliet's activities in the bedroom.

Tommy often told stories of the practical jokes played on the cast by Nervo and Knox during the run of that revue. They were always up to some trick or other. The one that amused him most was the time they nailed the slippers of a male dancer to the floor. This unfortunate target of their humour wore only a leopard

C

skin on the stage, and always left his slippers in the
wings when he leapt into the limelight bare-footed to
do his act. One can imagine the look on his face when
he came gliding off after taking his calls and stepped
into his slippers to walk to his dressing-room !

On another occasion in the same show, when the
company were all on the stage together as a troupe of
performing acrobats, the big man bent down so that
the others could jump on to his back. Suddenly Nervo
tripped forward, holding an egg which he dropped down
the back of the poor fellow's singlet, and proceeded to
follow this up by giving him a hearty slap on the back.
Of course the audience thought this was all part of the
fun and yelled with laughter, not knowing that the
grimaces of the victim were perfectly genuine. Never
in the history of that show did an actor make such
quick time from stage to dressing-room as Nervo did
that night, and he did not appear again until the curtain
was due to go up at the next performance, by which
time everybody, including the egged one, had seen the
joke.

" The Whirl of the World " was a very successful
show. It had a good run. It brought Tommy to the
year 1924—a historic year for him, for it marked his
first broadcast.

CHAPTER VII

HIS INTRODUCTION TO SAVOY HILL

IT would be easy to say that Tommy's début on the
air was an historic event that convinced him that
he had found his perfect medium, and that the listening
audience instantly recognised that the first big star of
radio had arrived. This was not the case, for the first
occasion on which he spoke into a B.B.C. microphone
was merely a relay—of the Royal Command Performance
of 1924 when " The Disorderly Room " was one of the
acts included in the show. Not many people, even
those whose memories go back to those days, will realise
what a modest sized audience even the Royal Command
show would have on the air. The British Broadcasting
Company, financed by about 1,700 shareholders connected with radio firms, had come into being in December,
1922. Offices and studios were taken in Magnet House,
Kingsway, and Marconi House, Strand. By March, 1923,
the Company was told that the L.C.C. Medical Headquarters in Savoy Hill were being moved, and they took
over a section of the building for studios and offices.

In October, 1922, there were 30,000 licensed listeners
(and probably an equal number of small boys listening
in with crystal sets), and by the time of Tommy's first
relay, the figure had increased to a million. On the
whole, the variety profession did not realise the great
El Dorado waiting for development. Partly this was
due to the alarm of the old-type comedian who found

that his jokes failed dismally when put over without the infectious glamour of the stage and the audience. More than that, it killed his act—and some of these old-timers had been saying the same thing twice nightly for two or three decades. Yet a few pioneers were showing what could be done. John Henry, a Yorkshire comedian, who told of his tribulations with his wife Blossom, was probably the first big name in radio variety. He succeeded because he gave fresh material every week and created a mental picture of himself in the listener's mind. There were others proving that special material for broadcasting could lift the somewhat turgid programmes right out of the rut. A case in point was with the first specially written musical comedy, Ernest Bullock's " The Dogs of Devon." When it was first transmitted in 1924 it brought in 5,000 ecstatic letters of praise—a total not beaten by the big outside broadcast of that year—the relay of the opening by King George V of the Empire Exhibition at Wembley. While radio history was being made, Tommy was busy with all kinds of special acts and sketches on provincial tours, including, of course, " The Disorderly Room," and great was his surprise when he received an invitation from the B.B.C. to go along for an audition. Jimmy Lester, producer of an old revue, " Dancing Time," in which he had made a brief appearance, stopped him in the street one day and told him that he was producing revues for the radio at Savoy Hill. " Come and sing a song for me," he invited. So Tommy went along to the little studio on the top floor of Savoy Hill. Jimmy explained that he would go into the next room to listen, and he told Tommy to start singing as soon as the red light went on. " When you've finished, just say something funny so that we can test your speaking voice," he added.

Tommy was left alone in the studio whose walls were covered in drapes, and faced the large contraption which housed the microphone on a stand. He started singing " I Had a Little Garden." Then he realised that the red light was still on and the time had come to say something funny. Every story he knew had disappeared ; every line of patter which seemed so natural when there was an audience out front seemed futile when all that was there was four blank walls and an electrical gadget. Time was passing, so he said : " Thirty days hath September, April, June and November . . ." He could not think how to go on, so he just said the first two lines again. Then he stopped, hesitated and added : " I can't remember the rest—go and work it out for yourselves."

Jimmy Lester came in roaring with laughter. It was not at what he said, but the way he said it, Jimmy explained. Tommy's desperate efforts to think of something funny had succeeded. This was a great relief, of course, to Tommy, and he was glad to know that he had not made quite such a fool of himself as he believed—or maybe he made a much greater fool than he had hoped. Despite the reaction of the B.B.C. staff he still believed that he had made his first and last attack on the microphone. He was astounded, therefore, when a few days later he received an invitation to broadcast. This brought new worry—what was he going to do over the ether ? People could not see him —so it entirely depended on what he said.

Up to this point there had been nothing really outstanding in Tommy's career. It had followed the usual line ; the rather mischievous schoolboy with a penchant for dressing up, the youth with a voice and certain gifts of comic invention becoming stage-struck. It had all happened a hundred times before. Nor had his stage career from chorus boy in " The Maid of the Mountains " through Concert Party and Revue to the Music Halls given any indication of future fame. There was no " star " quality in his work ; he was a pleasant, likeable but rather undistinguished performer, and I always felt that had he believed that one day he would reach the top, he would not have played " The Disorderly Room " so long—in fact the constant repetition of this somewhat out-moded sketch definitely did him harm.

Although he did not recognise it at the time his B.B.C. audition at Savoy Hill marked the turning point in his career. He was still to tour the Halls, still to display the decrepit Disorderly Room, but he was now for the first time heading for stardom thanks to his first visit to Savoy Hill. Apart too from his success in his audition, he was *liked* by the producers there, all of whom were pioneers. There was something different about him ; he was not a stage star condescending to try out the new medium ; he had no big ideas as to his ability to conquer it ; he was a quiet, friendly, humorous fellow who took direction easily and though as nervous then as he was a quarter of a century later he never let the show down. His Liverpool accent was much more pronounced then than in later years. He never entirely lost it, but his enunciation was clear ; he could make practically anything sound funny, and could enhance his lines with a variety of funny noises. He was, in fact, a born radio comedian who by a lucky chance was in at the birth of radio.

Again fortune smiled at him, for amongst the most popular and successful performers at Savoy Hill was a young singer, Jean Allistone, whom Tommy was to marry later on. She was rather better known in stage circles than he was. She was a star in her own right—the leading lady in a succession of Wylie and Tate, Firth Shepherd and Sir Alfred Butt's musical comedies—gifted with good looks, a beautiful singing voice and a speaking voice whose charm remains to this day. Whether it was love at first sight or not I've never discovered, but their marriage was one of the first studio romances and, in Tommy's subsequent success, she played a principal part. They were in " Radio Radiance " together in 1925 and in many other early B.B.C. successes. After her marriage to Tommy, Jean seldom broadcast but devoted all her time to his well-being. Self-effacingly from then onwards she shared in his career.

It was about this time, too, that he came under the personal management of Julius Darewski, who was his friend and mentor for so many years.

His success in " Radio Radiance " brought him a booking for its subsequent broadcasts, and it was about this time that I met him.

CHAPTER VIII

OUR ASSOCIATION BEGINS

IN these days I was still a " cat's-whisker " listener—
the new valve sets then on the market were beyond
my means. A cat's whisker, or crystal set, could of
course be made by anyone for a few shillings. It consisted of a crystal costing about sixpence, a wiggly wire
and a set of ear-phones. You simply touched the crystal
with the wire (or whisker) adjusted your head-phone,
and you got perfect sound—provided of course that no
one was reading a newspaper near by, for the mere
unfolding of a paper produced a noise greater than any
thunderstorm. My own set was housed in a cigar box
—not that I was smoking cigars that year, but it was
a convenient carrier for the crystal and the whisker.
I listened a lot, and the name of Tommy Handley
was vaguely familiar to me.

I had just got back from a trip to New Zealand and
Australia, working my passage as a ship's writer, and
was looking round for something to do. I had been
writing for some years, serious stuff mostly semi-scientific,
and had returned with some commissions to write occasional columns for Dominion papers, but since my
student days in Auckland and at Edinburgh—where I
had contributed what I then thought were highly comical
articles to the University Magazine—I had never at-
tempted anything even vaguely humorous. Listening
to 2LO as the London station was then known, it

occurred to me that someone must fashion the material
for broadcasting and that here was an outlet for a writer,
so I determined to have a go.

It happened that year that the Cup Final, the Boat
Race and the Grand National all took place within the
same fortnight, and this gave me an idea. If a man
dashed home on the Saturday afternoon to listen to the
Cup Final he might go to sleep and get the whole three
mixed up. I wrote up this idea in about 1,500 words
and sent it to Savoy Hill. Almost by return of post I
had a reply—they liked the idea, but could not use it
as written. However, for the idea alone would I accept
a fee of three guineas? Would I accept? In my state
of wealth at that time three guineas was a fortune!
I agreed without hesitation, and at once got to work
on other ideas, all of which were turned down. Apparently my future did not lie in Savoy Hill, and a visit
to what was then the Holy of Holies of Broadcasting
did little to reassure me. A suave young man there
pointed to a small filing cabinet and told me that it
was no use submitting ideas—in that cabinet they had
all they wanted. I must have felt, as I crawled out
on hands and knees, rather like Collie Knox did when
they told him he would never make a good announcer.
He stumbled blindly to the Embankment while I, having
now gained the perpendicular, staggered into the Coal
Hole, which was a great gathering place for the hier-
archy of Savoy Hill. I did not know one of them, and
drank my half-pint in solitude. Little did they know—
these big-wigs of broadcasting—that the pale, emaciated
figure in the corner, the red-haired man with the hang-
dog look would, years later, have *his* photo in the *Radio
Times*. Ha-ha-ha-*ha*-ha, as the wily woodpecker would
have cried!

Yet—this was not the end, for the very next day, when it was my wife's turn with the head-phones, she shouted : " They're doing that thing that *you* wrote," and tearing the 'phones off her head with large portions of hair attached, I heard my three guineas' epic being broadcast by Tommy Handley. Sensation in the combined room which was then the habitat of the Kavanagh *père, mère et fils* ! Moreover, this Handley bloke did it just as it was written, and he made it sound funny. Verily here was a man who must be met and wooed into accepting other equally comical scripts.

I found that he was appearing at the Holborn Empire, so I set forth to see him. I sent in my name—a name which meant nothing to him of course—and he came to the stage door to meet me. He proved to a dapper, pleasant-looking, friendly fellow dressed in Officer's Uniform—for of course he was appearing in " The Disorderly Room." I told him I was the writer of his recent broadcast, and he told me that the producer and others at Savoy Hill were delighted with it. Could I write some more ? He had no material of his own, he said, and wasn't creative in that way. So we arranged to meet again the next day, and there and then began an association which was destined to last until 1949.

By this time broadcasting had really caught on. Studios and relay stations were being opened up in the provinces, and each area had a far more highly individualistic programme than is the case to-day. Calls for broadcasts came in thick and fast, and despite the forebodings of the old school. Tommy soon proved that radio fame increased music hall bookings as well. He probably never had a busier time than in this period of the middle nineteen-twenties. He played in revues, he entertained in vaudeville, and new material had to be found for each. He would dash off to Weston-super-Mare to broadcast in a hospital carnival, or up to Manchester or Liverpool for a broadcast and a visit to his mother. He would do a quick show from the Edinburgh studios and then get across to Belfast for an evening's work in that station's programme. Often he was broadcasting in London while a Regional station was telephoning him for rehearsal dates.

Tommy, of course, became extremely well-known to everyone at Savoy Hill. In more recent years he often used to sigh for the pleasantly informal ways of those times. Producers, superintendents, engineers, and artistes, were members of one large and very happy family. There was, of course, none of the present page boy escorting, visitors' book signing, and so on. Tommy used to tell the story of the day that the Savoy Hill commissionaire was away for some reason, and a temporary man had taken his place. Tommy walked towards the door at the back of the entrance hall, when the new man stopped him and asked him what his business was. Such a thing had never happened before, and Tommy was rather taken aback for a moment.

" Are you a member of the staff, sir ? " the flunkey asked.

Tommy was unable to think of any particularly witty retort, so he said that he was.

" What department, may I ask ? "

This time he was equal to the occasion. He looked the man full in the eye and said : " Parligations and Merry Designs."

" Thank you very much, sir," replied the commissionaire, writing something in his book. Tommy often wondered what he put down.

There came a break for a short while in these

broadcasts when Tommy was engaged to tour with a farce called " Nerves." The show opened at the King's Theatre, Edinburgh. The first act had a mysterious Indian mooching on and off the stage, calling out what the author doubtless considered a suitably Oriental word—" Poo-nah ! " Meantime mysterious noises came from the other side of a large iron-studded door. In the second act on that opening night one of the characters said a line which was the cue to bring on another character—which in turn was the cue for the second act curtain. The stage hands obediently started to lower it, though the act had been going for less than ten minutes. Tommy started *ad libbing* in a loud voice to give a warning and bring the play back a few lines so that everyone could make a fresh start. The curtain stopped, reversed and went up again. The dialogue continued nicely until they reached the same point— and once again the culprit gave the same wrong cue. This time the curtain came down and stayed down. There was nothing to be done about it, and the third act was started, with none of the audience knowing what on earth the story was about. At the *finale* there was hardly any applause, and Tommy was asked to go out and explain what had happened. It says something for his ability to explain the whole thing away that at the end the audience gave him a rousing round of applause and then trooped out of the theatre perfectly content with their evening's entertainment—although it had only lasted about an hour and a half.

Next night the play went all right until the mysterious Indian did his piece. The big thrill of his act in front of the iron-studded door came when he opened it and dragged out a donkey. At rehearsal the animal had obediently stepped towards the footlights. This night it refused to budge, and the sequence was a weird mixture of " Poon-ah !—come on out, duckie, come on out, there's a good lad—Poon-ah !—come on out of it, you so-and-so—Poo-nah ! "

When the show moved to the Borough Theatre, Stratford, the manager decided that the donkey was too risky, and that the noises behind the door might just as well come from a parrot. A guaranteed reliable bird was obtained, but unfortunately it took a strong dislike to Poo-nah. When he carried it on to the stage on a wooden perch, the bird sidled slowly on to his arm and fixed a beady eye on his ear.

The audience heard the following dialogue : " Poo-nah—you stay away from me, you brute—Poo-nah !—you wait till I get you outside—Poonah ! " Then came the inevitable yell of agony. A scene of high Eastern drama lapsed into comedy, and was, in the audience's opinion, by far the best part of the show.

" Nerves " lasted six weeks, and was Tommy's last attempt at farce. As soon as he returned to London Tommy had a big radio job—commentator on the 1927 Royal Command Show. He admits that this was one of the times when he felt something approaching mike-fright. Everyone is on edge for this show, the biggest event of the Variety calendar. He stood in the wings at the Victoria Palace so that he could see something of both sections of the house. He took up his position about a quarter of an hour before the show was due to begin, and he had a bell-push to let the engineers under the stage know when there was something in the theatre on which to commentate.

The stage manager explained : " I'll stand in the wings on the other side, and when I get the word that the King and Queen are in the foyer, I'll wave my hand. Then you can start your preliminary patter, and by the time you've finished the King and Queen will be in the Royal Box and the show will be ready to start." The manager duly waved his hand, and Tommy began his prepared commentary, for which I had written gags about all the artistes. He got to the end of it, and there was still no sign of the Royal patrons. He started to improvise and ran out of patter again. There was still no sign. He carried on once more— and after what seemed an interminable time Their Majesties appeared. Tommy had started broadcasting when the stage manager raised his hand to flick some fluff off the curtains !

There was another incident in this show which, though it did not come off, indicates the generous spirit which always pervaded Tommy when he could give a helping hand to fellow artistes. There was naturally a chorus in the programme, and their speciality dance was given just before the interval at nine o'clock. Tommy had memorised the names of all the girls in the chorus, and we had prepared a series of gags on each one, so that he could lighten the broadcast of an act which was merely musical. The girls came on to the stage, and he began his patter. The stage manager came up and gripped his elbow. "Just what," he asked, " do you think you are doing ? "

Tommy waved him angrily away, afraid the listeners would hear the interruption.

" The mike's dead, my good Tom ! " he said. " The show's running late. They're transmitting the news now ! "

There was one strange sequel from this Command commentary. A day or so later someone got in touch with Tommy and said : " I understand you're very good at telling amusing anecdotes. I'd like you to come to a dinner party at my place on Friday and entertain my guests after dinner. It's a little way outside London. I'll send a car ; of course you'll stay the night—and, er, I thought a fee of fifty pounds ? "

Tommy not unnaturally agreed that he might be free on the night in question.

"That's fine," said the stranger. "Just one point : I don't want you to appear as an engaged artiste, but disguised as a friend of mine."

Tommy was duly collected in a limousine and shown to a room in a magnificent country house. At dinner —a truly splendid meal—he was put near his host, and when they came to the brandy and cigars, Tommy whispered to his host : "Shall I start telling some stories now ? "

The guest on the other side overheard him. "Speaking of stories," he said, "have you heard the one about . . . ? "

Other guests were reminded of their best anecdotes. It went on for hours. Every time Tommy tried to start he was interrupted. He did not tell a single story.

Next morning he met his host before breakfast. He had a cheque for £50 in his hand. Tommy said that he had certainly not earned it. "My dear chap," protested the other, " it was you who started them off. It was the most successful dinner I've ever given. And you're responsible."

It was not often that audiences were so easily pleased.

CHAPTER IX

THE YEARS BETWEEN

TOMMY had by this time reached a position in the variety and radio world where innumerable people approached him for his co-operation in various ways where his fame and ability to entertain would be helpful. He was, in fact, as near the state of " social lion " as his homely North Country character would ever allow him to get. One of the most unusual of these private appearances was in 1927. He had a telephone call from Sir Henry Wood, who asked Tommy if he could manage to come along to his home and help him entertain a group of old ladies. Sir Henry gave this party every summer at his lovely house near Chorley Wood, or rather in the magnificent studio which had been largely built by the conductor, even to the laying of the fine dance floor it contained.

When Tommy arrived the party had been going for some time, and after tea Tommy gave them a few minutes of extempore patter. He then said he thought they might like him to sing, and they asked him for two of their favourites—Tommy's then famous " Pink Plant Pot " and the current 1927 hit, " Constantinople." To his surprise and maybe embarrassment Sir Henry jumped up from his chair and said he would accompany Tommy on the piano. He gave the only rendering that the simple melody of " Pink Plant Pot " would allow, and then began on " Constantinople." He liked this errand boy's jingle very much, for oblivious of his audi-

The Mayor of Foaming-at-the-Mouth is menaced by Funf (Jack Train)

Handley's Half Hour
(Dorothy Carless and Doreen Villiers discuss the script with Producer
Pat Dixon and Tommy)

Edward G. Robinson "reaches for the sky"

Tommy in one of the many radio pantomimes he appeared in during
the war. He is the simple schoolboy on the left
(Derek McCulloch—Uncle Mac—is introducing Dorothy Summers
(Mrs. Mopp) to the children)

In the early days of *Variety Bandbox* Tommy appears with Bing Crosby

Sherlock Handley seeks a clue in
Dr. Watson's moustache

Well! I'll sip from the saucer!
This *is* a nice cup of tea

H. A. Summers, Keynsham

Clifton Parish Hall, Bristol, where *Itma* was born

Tommy takes a pre-peep at the script
(Tommy, Ted Kavanagh and Francis Worsley)

"I like that one, but what will the Censor say?"

"We can't do any more to the script. Let's sleep on it!"

Itma, it was said, was inverted logic!

Old Gaffer Handley, one-time
Squire of Much Fiddling. 1944

Sam Scram (Sydney Keith)
prepares Tommy for his first
broadcast to the Army

"I've brought this for you, sir"
Mrs. Mopp (Dorothy Summers) makes one of her many offerings

What a card! Tommy with Lind Joyce, Diana Morrison (Miss Hotchkiss), and Jean Capra (Naieve)

ence, he played it over and over again. Tommy sang the chorus the first time round, and then he joined the audience while the best-known conductor of his era turned a rather pointless music hall tune into something stirring and beautiful. The old ladies sat spellbound at the world-famous musician making the old rafters ring with " Constantinople." An hour later he left to conduct a " Prom " at the Queen's Hall.

Tommy now began to star in his own radio revues. The first one was " Inaninn," one of the very early radio parties which have been copied in one version or another ever since. After that came " Handley's Manœuvres," " Tommy's Tours," and " Hot Pot." They were new experiments in radio presentation, and broke new ground. Sometimes there were amusing errors in their production.

In one of these revues there was a short sketch—a serious thriller. The climax of the action was the sacrifice of the heroine's life for her lover. Just as the villain drew a gun to shoot his rival, the noble girl adroitly stepped between them and received the bullet in her own charming chassis. Sound effects were not what they are to-day, and the only way the thud of the falling body could be broadcast was by the microphone picking up the sound of the body really falling. The villain, who in real life was something of a Sir Galahad, volunteered to do this for the girl, which seemed reasonable enough. Unfortunately the producer had forgotten about the studio audience. When the Heavy fired the gun at the girl and promptly fell down dead himself, they roared with laughter. The B.B.C.'s mail bag was pretty full the next day with enquiries as to what was funny about this tragic scene.

Another very popular series on the B.B.C. at this period was the Surprise Item, forerunner of " In Town To-night." Novelty was the angle that the originator,

John Macdonnell, was always looking for, and knowing the private reputation Tommy had as a singer he asked him to come along and give a straight song. Tommy sang " The Driver of the 8.15," and his name was not given until the end. Listeners' letters afterwards were divided roughly into two parts—those who thought the whole thing was a fake, and those who regretted that a man with such a fine voice didn't throw up everything for a career on the concert platform. So far as I know, this was the only time Tommy sang in serious vein, though a recording has occasionally been broadcast as a novelty. He had a voice of remarkable range as he proved in his impersonation of Malcolm MacEachern (Jetsam). Had he not become a famous comedian, he could have always earned a living as a singer.

The B.B.C. did, however, give Tommy plenty of opportunity to sing his comic songs. Some of his most successful efforts in this regard in pre-war days were in pantomimes. He took part in several of them, the first being " Cinderella " in the Savoy Hill era. It was, of course, an Ernest Longstaffe show. Tommy played Buttons, and Jean Allistone was again in a show with Tommy, playing the lead.

None of the cast at either that broadcast or any of the others in which they appeared together had any idea that there was a romance in progress. I myself, who was sharing Tommy's flat, did not realise that a marriage was in the offing. Then one evening, as we were walking around the West End as we often did, he said casually : " By the way, Ted, are you doing anything particular to-morrow morning ? "

" No, I don't think so," I replied. " Why ? "

" Oh well, I thought that you might like to come along and be best man—Jean and I are getting married."

I was told not to tell anyone—and I kept my word until after the event. So far as I know only the officials and Tommy's mother had any idea that Tommy had that morning resigned from bachelorhood.

It was a quiet wedding, with only a few close friends in attendance followed by lunch at the Holborn Restaurant. Off they went to spend a few days—all that their broadcasting dates would allow—at the Old Ship Hotel, Brighton, from where I will always remember Jean wrote me a long and very amusing letter which I kept until all my scripts and papers were destroyed in the Blitz in 1940. As soon as they had gone, I 'phoned the Press, and within an hour posters announcing a " Radio Romance " were all over the place —including Brighton. Both Jean and Tommy were fond of Brighton and spent their last holiday together there in the summer of 1948—this time at the Queen's Hotel where Tom Clarke, who had been Manager of the Savage for so long, was now in charge. He told me recently that Tommy dreaded going back to London to start his new ITMA series in September. Already he must have felt that he had not much longer to go.

After his brief honeymoon, Tommy returned to take part in a Radio variety show, and as he walked on the stage for his act Jack Payne's band played Lohengrin's " Wedding March." Tommy's secret wedding was out with a vengeance. There was another charming gesture to come. After the show Tommy was handed a small package. Inside was a gold cigarette case inscribed :

TOMMY HANDLEY
19TH FEBRUARY, 1929
WITH ALL GOOD WISHES
FROM THE
B.B.C.

During his career Tommy received several offers for film work. He had been approached to make a talking film as early as 1925, more than two years before Al Jolson's " Singing Fool " swept silent pictures away for good. He had a voice test, was given full marks and told to stand by for a call. When it came he was on tour and, like the opportunity of joining the D'Oyly Carte Gilbert and Sullivan company, he had to refuse an offer which might have changed his whole career.

Few people believed Tommy when he told them of this early talkie venture, but it is down in cinema history, though soft-pedalled by U.S. reference books, which like to show that they were first in the field. The studio was at Clapham. It had been a cinema as far back as 1907, and was taken over in 1925 for the production of Lee De Forest Phonofilms. It was about the worst possible place for a sound film studio that anyone could have found. It stood in the shadow of a railway bridge over which electric and steam trains roared day and night to the Junction of world-wide fame. There were stables adjoining, and Tommy's own voice test was ruined by the neighing of a horse.

The studio had only one camera and one lens. The stage equipment consisted of two banks of mercury lamps and a couple of ancient spotlights. Every door had to be shut tight in an abortive attempt to keep out the train and stable noises. Temperatures soared to tropical heights during " takes." Under these conditions Tommy gave a humorous monologue, with the grease paint literally collecting in pools on his collar. And before the end, the horse neighed. He was convinced he had failed, though, as I say, the producers liked his test very much.

For the record and to show that this was no hair-brained scheme of an idealistic inventor, the Clapham studio did manage under these almost impossible conditions to turn out some quite presentable films. Owen Nares, Malcolm Keen, and Mary Clare appeared in them, and they were shown at the Wembley Exhibition in 1925, where for sixpence an hour of sound films was presented in what was probably the world's first exclusively talkie palace.

Later Tommy made some comedy films, though it must be admitted that, like most British pictures of that era, they were too cheaply made to exploit him as they could have done with really good presentation, and they were soon forgotten. After this experience, Tommy rightly decided to leave the cinema to others, but there was one most successful contribution which he gave to film humour—the commentaries on the series of re-issued Chaplin comedies which had, of course, been made as silent films. Tommy said that this was one of the most difficult jobs he ever tackled. The films depended on a tremendous number of flash-backs for their narrative content, action was terrifically fast, and time had to be gauged for the audience's laughter. But this experiment of letting Britain's premier sound comic explain the antics of Hollywood's greatest visual comic was entirely successful. I had already penetrated the film world, writing trailers and commentaries, and was familiar with the technique. I helped him with the commentary he did for " Tilly's Punctured Romance," and then write the commentary for the six silent Chaplins. Although they were half an hour in length Tommy, with the aid of one " effects " man, did each in one morning—a run-through and then the recording. So rapid was his delivery and so sure his touch that he was able to do this without a " fluff," and although they were made so many years ago, they are as popular as ever to-day.

Tommy was to make more ambitious films later on, but he was now what the Americans would call " big time." He toured his own radio show for two years— one of the first on the road to exploit the popularity of artistes who had gained fame via the microphone. He also toured for two years with a very successful show called " Hello, Folks ! " which was, by the way, given a special relay from the Palace, Blackpool, as part of the B.B.C.'s New Year's festivities on January 1st, 1931.

All this time Tommy's radio programmes were basic- ally solo efforts, but in 1934 came a notable meeting which resulted in a new radio act—Mr. Murgatroyd and Mr. Winterbottom—himself and Ronald Frankau, whose career had some remarkable parallels with Tommy's own life. Both had been through the pro- verbially hard school of experience. Ronald Frankau, like Tommy, lost his father while he was still a child, though there was a great difference in childhood en- vironment. His mother was a well-known novelist (Frank Danby), and his father left a prosperous cigar business, immortalised in Ronald's elder brother, Gilbert Frankau's novel " Peter Jackson, Cigar Merchant." Ronald was at Eton while Tommy was going to his day school in Liverpool. While Tommy was running mes- sages for a pram firm, Ronald was studying to become a business executive. One had to make his way as the uninfluential Tommy Handley ; the other was told to get ahead without the help of the family name, as Frank Ronalds. During the war both were in service concert parties—Tommy with the R.N.A.S. and Ronald in the " Morse-key Toes " with a company composed of signallers out in Mesopotamia. After the war, while

Tommy was entertaining people at Bognor and Llandrindod Wells, Ronald was doing the same thing on the pier at Eastbourne.

By 1924 Ronald was running five concert parties, headed by the " Cabaret Kittens." In 1927, the year that Tommy gave his Royal Command commentary, Ronald made his radio debut with " The Kittens." It seems only right that these two, with a wealth of knowledge of the modern form of quick-fire topical patter, should one day join forces.

They first got together in 1930 in an act called " North and South." Tommy was very Lancastrian and Ronald all that the public thought an old Etonian should be. They used to do a bit of patter and finish up with a popular song of the day—often " The Stein Song " or " Down on Misery Farm."

The Murgatroyd-Winterbotham act emerged from this. They both went along to see Eric Maschwitz, then head of the B.B.C. Variety Department, and told him that they had thought out a new type of comedy act—a simple one of having two comics instead of one funny man and a foil. It first went on the air in December, 1934, and proved a constant trump card for the variety producers.

It was a remarkable achievement for both actors —a complete change from their solo acts. The B.B.C. always regarded them as an act all on their own for these appearances—even the administrative departments used to make out their contracts and cheques in the names of Mr. Murgatroyd and Mr. Winterbotham.

On the first occasion that the act was broadcast the name appeared in the *Radio Times* and daily press programmes as Winterbotham. Less than a week after

the show Tommy received the following letter from a
gentleman of that name :

" Sir,—Are you aware that the name of Winterbotham
is one which is borne by a very old family, of which I
am a member ? I feel that the use to which you have
put it has done little to enhance its reputation, and
shall be greatly obliged if you will have the goodness
to discontinue its publication in this connection. Otherwise I shall be compelled to take legal action."

Tommy wrote humbly to say that he had never intended any insult, and would his correspondent mind
if he spelled it Winterbottom, as he had originally intended ? Back came a reply to say that with this change
everything would be quite all right.

The scripts of the Murgatroyd-Winterbottom sketches
are gems of punning gone mad, as can be seen from
the following extract from a commentary on the Oxford-
Cambridge boat-race. It is interesting to realise, from
reading this, what an enormous asset is the timing of
two experienced artists :

TOMMY : Well, what shall we talk about ?
RONALD : About seven and half minutes. Let's talk
about affairs of the whirled.
TOMMY : Yes—take the humming top.
RONALD : What's that got to do with it ?
TOMMY : Well, it's a whirled affair.
RONALD : We've got to tighten our belts.
TOMMY : I only wear braces. Think of sugar.
RONALD : I do—and a lump comes in my throat.
Actually there's enough corn raised . . .
TOMMY : To cover every toe in England—and that
will spoil the Pilgrim's progress.
RONALD: That's Bunyan. Do you know there's enough food
in the world for every man, woman and child.

TOMMY : Cat and dog life—but I'm a little hoarse.

RONALD : Nay.

TOMMY : All right, I will. (*Neighs.*)

RONALD : Which reminds me—with the elimination of horses, leather merchants can't get a meal for a tanner.

TOMMY : And blacksmiths are working on farms shooing geese.

RONALD : It's propaganda that's wanted—can you wonder that all the farmers are going about with rye faces ?

TOMMY : *Amaz*-ing.

RONALD : Well, they've " Barley " enough to live on.

TOMMY : They are all right then—but even the barbers are complaining about their crops.

RONALD : They've shingle-track minds. But there certainly is a permanent wave of discontent.

TOMMY : It's all a sham ! Pooh, I remember the time potatoes were a penny a peck.

RONALD : Now they are a flash in the pan. In a crisis the world wants to look round.

TOMMY : It always has been.

RONALD : Talking shop—how does your wife get on with the ration book ?

TOMMY : She knows it all from A to Z—crosses the T's and dots the eyes of anyone who tries to take her place.

RONALD : Like my wife—she just looks after her vegetables and waits.

TOMMY : I don't get it.

RONALD : She minds her P's and Q's.

TOMMY : I like that ! Do you know—I dared to tell my butcher off the other day.

RONALD : You must have some guts !

TOMMY : No, *he* had them, and *I* wanted them.

RONALD : I see—inside information.

TOMMY : Don't talk tripe. I've hardly got any bacon now.

RONALD : Jolly hard cheese.

TOMMY : Oh, I get that—it's the frost.

RONALD : Our nurse got into trouble the other day for fetching a hundredweight of coal in a pram.

TOMMY : What's wrong with that?

RONALD : Well, she forgot to take the baby out first.

TOMMY : What an anthracite for sore eyes! I suppose you gave her the sack, and now you've got to get a new nurse?

RONALD : No, a new baby. Of course you've got central heating—are your pipes always hot?

TOMMY : No—I've given up smoking.

RONALD : Smoking apart—let's buy a boat and emigrate.

TOMMY : Don't talk bilge water—by the way, do you know anything about vessels?

RONALD : Blood or drinking.

TOMMY : No. I mean those things that women and children get off first.

RONALD : Ah, men's knees.

TOMMY : No, boats.

RONALD : Have you ever been aboard?

TOMMY : A board? There should be a good three ply to that. No, not lately.

RONALD : Well, the schooner the better. Surely you have at least been in a wherry?

TOMMY : Ferry often. I've been in a very merry wherry ferry.

RONALD : Oh, a jolly boat—who rowed?

TOMMY : Gordon Richards. Have you ever been piped aboard?

RONALD : Oh, much better than that, I've been cigared.

TOMMY : Not with abandon?

RONALD : No. I had to stand at the end of a Cuba— I smuggled a soprano called Florence aboard. She tried to reach some high notes at the ship's concert.

TOMMY : Oh ! She sang for her scupper—did she get much applause ?

RONALD : As a matter of fact she was clapped in irons.

TOMMY : For defaulting on the high seas—did she take many calls ?

RONALD : Too many—so the Captain put a shot across her bows—poor Florence. Do you know what he finally said to her ?

TOMMY : Yes—Scapa Floe.

RONALD : That's right.

TOMMY : I have a nephew who's a matelot. You know what a matelot is ?

RONALD : A thing you get on your finger.

TOMMY : What a wit-low comedy I call it. My nephew sailed the Seven and a half Seas.

RONALD : There are only seven.

TOMMY : Are there ? Well he was always half seas over. What are the Seven Seas ?

RONALD : Well—there's the Baltic.

TOMMY : The Caribbean.

RONALD : The Red Sea.

TOMMY : The Tennessee.

RONALD : The B.B.C.

TOMMY : The wait and See.

RONALD : Dolly Elsie.

TOMMY : D.S.O.

RONALD : D.S.O. ?

TOMMY : Sorry—the M.C.

RONALD : *Ici on parle Français.*

TOMMY : North Sea.

RONALD : South Sea.

TOMMY : Portsmouth.

RONALD : And all stations to Littlehampton. Did you ever go on a cruise before the war ?

TOMMY : Yes, but I came back.

RONALD : Where did you go—Norway ?

TOMMY : No, I went the other way.

RONALD : I went on a cruise, too.
TOMMY : Oh, two crews.
RONALD : Yes—Oxford and Cambridge.

In April, 1934, a broadcast in a cavalcade of variety, " The First Twelve Years "—his own act in a series of Radiolympia shows for three years' running (including his appearance from a hansom cab in the spectacular " In Town To-night " stage show), the respected head-master of St. Basil's School in Harry S. Pepper's " The White Coons " in the early thirties, innumerable variety appearances, spots in the Children's Hour . . . the complete record of Tommy's radio work in those days would need a far larger book than this.

But there is one broadcast which deserves special mention, partly because it signified the first professional meeting between Tommy and Francis Worsley, producer of the ITMA shows, then talks producer at Bristol. Francis was put in charge of an outside broadcast from the Cheddar Caves. He considered that a straight talk about the caves, their formation, history, and so on might seem a trifle dull to a public which was at that time writing plenty of rude letters to the Press about interminable lectures on the air, while every comic could raise a laugh by referring to a B.B.C. talk on the miracles of pond life.

The experts who were to explain the geological matters were human enough to agree that a little leavening of the subject would certainly not come amiss, and it was arranged that Tommy should accompany the party going round the caves, with *carte blanche* to chip in now and then with remarks to the guide.

Tommy wrote and asked me to send him a script, so I got hold of a guide book and worked out some appropriate gags. Tommy started off with the party, and when they came to the cave known as Aladdin's, Tommy remarked that if a pantomime were ever performed there no doubt the principal boy would wear stalactights. There seemed nothing in bad taste about this either to Tommy or myself, and after all a gagster knows no shame, and the programme engineers were not sufficiently horrified to cut him off the air.

Francis Worsley also went home with the feeling that the job had been done quite well. Unfortunately events proved that Tommy had annoyed the Lord Mayor of Nottingham. When the British Association met in that town a few days later, he said : " It is disgraceful that the stalagmites and stalactites of the Cheddar Caves should have been made the butt of cheap music hall wit." This was, of course, Fleet Street's meat, and the reporters who blithely ignored all the profound scientific statements pouring out in a steady stream from the assembled brains at Nottingham played up the attack for all they were worth.

Tommy meekly stated : " I was engaged by the B.B.C. to do a humorous broadcast as a tourist in the caves, and naturally I tried to make my comment as amusing as possible. Far from deriding the caves, I think they are most beautiful. To ridicule them was the farthest thing from my mind."

This presumably let out Tommy, for the Mayor next turned his big guns on the poor producer, when he told the Press : " Whoever was responsible for the organisation of that part of the programme is guilty of extremely bad taste. I consider that those people who make the caves and gorge a subject of cheap wit have no sense of sanctity. The broadcast was, to my mind, desecration and senseless. They will be going into Westminster Abbey soon and poking fun at the men who are buried there."

Things were now going nicely—with plenty of publicity for everything from the fossilised bones of prehistoric animals found in the caves to Nottingham lace. The B.B.C.'s Press Department kept the ball rolling with a statement : " The programme consisted of first a serious description of the Gorge, followed by another serious description of the caves by a spelæologist—a specialist in caves. Tommy Handley, accompanied by a real guide, belonging to the caves, put a number of amusing questions. The broadcast was therefore a mixture of the serious and the comic. We are sorry that the Lord Mayor of Nottingham should have thought Tommy Handley an unwelcome addition to the party, and hope that other listeners liked him better."

Some of my Fleet Street friends were cynical enough to insinuate that either Tommy or I had engineered the whole thing as a publicity stunt. I had to explain that in our wildest dreams we couldn't have conjured up such a storm in a teacup, or crisis in a cave, and if we had we wouldn't have expected it to become front-page news.

But in that September 1937 twenty-four page papers were grateful for anything that could be played up into a good news feature. One year later they were to find all the news they wanted with words like " Sudetenland — Chamberlain — Munich." And twenty-four months later the Cheddar Caves were to become just somewhere safe for art treasures. The Years Between were over.

CHAPTER X

THE BIRTH OF ITMA

IN 1938 (Munich Year) Tommy's position in the radio world was a peculiar one. He had now been broadcasting regularly since the earliest days of Savoy Hill, and, of the pioneers, only he and Leonard Henry had maintained their lead in the comedy field. Popular though he was, however, the day of the solo comedian was fast declining, the comedy series was on its way and, so far, no series was in sight for him. He was not broadcasting as much as usual, most of his time was spent on tour, but he made regular appearances in B.B.C. Music Hall and various other single spots at frequent intervals. I knew that he felt that he had new fields to conquer, provided he found the right idea, but at the moment the appropriate medium eluded him.

Again, the B.B.C. had grown greatly since Savoy Hill days—the Variety Department now had vast ramifications, and in the comedy field a host of rivals sprang up. Competition increased and a new type of show was introduced—the idea of a series being the prevailing fashion. One must be found for Tommy, insisted John Watt who had now replaced Eric Maschwitz. Eric had resigned in order to devote himself to authorship and was destined to win international success with " Balalaika," " Paprika " and many other romantic musical comedies. Under Eric's guidance the Variety

95

Department flourished. His flair for entertainment amounted to genius, and his energy was colossal. He had the ability to inspire both his own staff and the artistes he engaged—he may well be called the Father of Variety as we know it to-day. With Charles Brewer as his first lieutenant the Variety Department had become one of the most active in the B.B.C., and, when John Watt took over, its growth was greatly accelerated. To these three—Maschwitz, Brewer and Watt—Tommy owed a good deal. Right through his career they had helped and encouraged him and remained his firm friends always. Later I will quote what Eric said about him— one of the best expressed of the many tributes paid to him by those amongst whom he spent his radio life.

It is difficult to-day to realise that in pre-war days the show-with-a-story was a radio novelty. "Band-waggon" pioneered the idea with the Wednesday night activities of Arthur Askey and Stinker Murdoch in their B.B.C. Flat. The planners at Broadcasting House were delighted to find that at last there was a show which seemed to please everybody. The order went out to start another series to be broadcast "same time, same station" every week, and Tommy was an obvious choice to play the lead. Over in America the same sort of formula for radio success had been discovered, with such stars as Amos an' Andy, Jack Benny, and Burns and Allen. Variety producers at the B.B.C. agreed that Tommy's almost unique gift was that of seemingly spontaneous quick-fire patter, and that he could certainly put over a show with all the speed and verve of a U.S. broadcast. Basically, the idea, and it was not a very good one, was to create an English version of the Burns and Allen show. Film-goers will know that this act is hardly a parallel of anything in which Tommy could appear. Bob Burns is a poker-faced, monosyllabic character, while Gracie Allen gives every indication—as Bob mentioned on one occasion—of being vaccinated with a gramophone needle. Any English show based on this sort of quick repartee act would obviously have to reverse the characters.

Celia Eddy, a Canadian actress, was to share the microphone with Tommy, and several scripts were prepared. Tommy didn't feel that any of them were suitable, and it was in the early summer of 1939 that he suggested I might come along with a few ideas. And so, with Francis Worsley the producer, and Tommy, we held the first of many story conferences one warm June afternoon in the Langham Hotel, the pre-war " wet canteen " of the B.B.C. just across the way from Broadcasting House, and now, regrettedly, a hotel no more. This was my first meeting with Francis, with whom I was destined to work so often in the ensuing years. At that time I was writing a series called " Lucky Dip " which had had a very long run, and in which I first met Jack Train and Dick Bentley, both of whom were to win radio fame in days to come. Jack was a newcomer to broadcasting, but showed that great promise which later on he was to fulfil. Dick, recently arrived from Australia, was building up considerable popularity which now, in 1949—ten years later, is greater than ever. I had not written anything for Tommy for some time, but it was typical of him that he had not forgotten me and that he sought my help when in need. The environment at that meeting in the Langham was right in harmony with the crazy character of the show we were devising. Somewhere or other there was a London conference on religious matters at that time, and the Langham had evidently been put on the list of approved

D

accommodation for the clerical delegates. Tommy, Francis and myself, therefore, sat at a small table amid a perfect hubbub of discussion on church matters, fortifying ourselves with large lagers as we wrestled with the script that had been provided and which had a distinct American flavour.

We at least had a title : " It's That Man Again ! " It was a 1938-1939 catch phrase which fitted any of the periodic rantings and ravings of the Führer in Berlin. The *Daily Express* ran the phrase as a headline every time the call for *Lebensraum* went up from the Third Reich, and people were saying it to one another in that half-fearful, half-amused manner which was a symptom of the queasy feeling that preceded the outbreak of war.

The scene of our new series was on board a ship, a sort of mad hatter's " Strength Through Joy " cruising vessel, in which Tommy would be in charge of the festivities. He would have Celia as his dumb blonde secretary nicknamed Cilly, and for no particular reason one of the passengers would be a mad Russian inventor named Vladivostooge, played by Eric Egan. That was the kernel of the show, and it says much for the B.B.C.'s faith in Tommy Handley as a reliable broadcaster that this sort of skit was, with reservations, approved by the administrative sections. It can well be imagined that with the whole of Europe like the proverbial tinder box the B.B.C. had to be very careful not to give offence. Even a slight deviation from the script might have caused another crisis, and would certainly have created a spate of letters from the usual indignant readers grinding the axes of their own pet " isms " of the period. But in all his career Tommy had never been known to extemporise through excitement or " artistic licence."

Jack Harris's Band from the London Casino was engaged for the music, with Pat Taylor as the singer. There were two features in the show—a " Guess or No " charade run by Lionel Gamlin and " Man Bites Dog " by Sam Heppner—in which mundane situations were reversed to give them audience appeal.

After a lot of work and discussion it was agreed that the general idea looked promising enough to warrant a short series, and the programme schedule gave six fortnightly shows through the summer season. The first one was to be from 8.15 p.m.–9 p.m. on Wednesday, July 12th.

The programme was broadcast from the large studio at Maida Vale. The first words that were said after the programme announcement came from Tommy. They were spoken on the telephone : " Hello ! Is that Turner, Turner and Turtle ? It is ? Then good morning, good morning, good morning, good morning. It's that man again. That's right, Tommy Handley ! "

It was quite a nice little show, and was followed by three more. There was a gap scheduled after this because Radiolympia was running from August 23rd onwards, and special broadcasts had been arranged for this period. We were down for a resumption of the cruise on September 5th. Needless to say, this edition never reached the air.

By early August Tommy, in common with other stalwarts of broadcasting and the B.B.C. staff, had received confidential orders on what they must do if a state of emergency should arise. Those in the know were told of a secret signal. As soon as the announcements preceding the news bulletin changed from " This is the National Programme " to " This is London," it meant that the key people were to make their way by any means at their disposal to Bristol. On that sunny Sunday morning of September 3rd he heard the sentence that was to send him packing off to Bristol, and he arrived the same night—to find this small regional centre of the B.B.C. a chaotic mess of hundreds of people all eager to see that the show went on—as indeed, from top level orders, it was officially ordained that it must.

Conditions for broadcasting were quite unfamiliar; security was of paramount importance, for it will be remembered that at the beginning of the war there were many rumours about ingenious systems of getting messages to the enemy via some innocent item. The stories ranged from simple pre-arranged codes based on words in talks to involved arrangements whereby a few piano notes revealed the entire movements of the British Navy to gentlemen wearing head-phones in a listening post in Bremen. They were all very silly, but there was, of course, a germ of possible sense in them. After all, Tommy and everyone else scrambling for billets in Bristol had come there by means of a radio code.

I was not with the advance party as I had not been chosen as a member of the Variety Repertory Company, but I had been given a hint to stand by should war break out. As I had not been " vetted " by the Home Office I could not write anything for broadcasting, but when a wire came from John Watt " Come at once " I knew I had passed scrutiny, and made my way to Bristol at once.

When I arrived I went straight to Francis Worsley's office, and found Tommy there. Francis had been taking a short holiday when war broke out, and considering his delayed arrival in Bristol—he had come all the way from his town in the Home Counties by taxi on September 3rd because someone had forgotten to tell him about the code signal—his office was not at all bad. It was in a study in one of the Houses of Clifton College. It was there that, with pictures of college sports teams still on the wall, that all three of us started plans for a new version of the show, having first chewed it over in the garden in Whiteladies Road where the B.B.C. canteen now stands.

Conferences were held at all hours of the day and night, for there had been a tremendous rush to get normal programmes going after a day or two of bulletins, gramophone records, and marathon performances by Sandy Macpherson on the organ. Tommy was appearing in almost every kind of light entertainment going out from Bristol, and Francis had two or three programmes a day to produce. To add to our difficulties, everyone lived two or three miles from everybody else. I shared a billet with Tommy, and we spent hours discussing the future.

The programme planners took the strong-arm method of simply stating that " It's That Man Again " would be broadcast on September 19th. They gave us thirty minutes, and a strong supporting cast—Jack Train, Maurice Denham, Vera Lennox, and Jack Hylton's Band, conducted by Billy Ternant, with Sam Costa as vocalist. Jack Train was not in the Variety Repertory Company, but I wired him and he came straight away.

It was obvious that the cruise idea would have to go. Holidays at sea were as *passé* as peace. Suddenly there was the strange outbreak of initials on every car on the road—the labels presumably being intended to get priority of passage. Everyone remembers the sort of thing : A.R.P., R.A.F., M.O.F., R.N.V.R., VET., W.V.S., W.D., and so on. Half the initials were private ideas born of pomposity and self-importance, and I

admired the girl who used to run around Bristol in an
old two-seater with a large label on the wind-screen
bearing the words " JUST ME."

There did, however, seem humorous possibilities in
this epidemic of abbreviations.   There was also the
phenomenon of gigantic Ministries which, though
planned secretly months before, seemed to the newspaper reader and listener to bloom overnight. After
every evening news bulletin came a spate of orders
issued by these Ministries.

And as it is the British temperament never to be
awed by such matters even though the greatest war of
all time was allegedly going to wipe their cities out in
a matter of a week or so, the trio planning the new
programme thought that the Ministry craze should get
some topical publicity too.

On scraps of paper the new Tommy Handley emerged
—as Minister of Aggravation and Mysteries, provided
with accommodation by courtesy of the Office of Twerps.

I can claim no credit for the title of the show.   It
caused a lot of brain-searching, for we knew that it
should certainly cash in on the initial vogue.   M.A.M.
was no good ; O.O.T. was hardly worth consideration ;
nothing could be done with T.H.   One day, while we
were racking our brains for something easy to say and
easy to remember, Tommy was doodling on the blotting
paper, as he usually did at our conferences. He wrote
out the name of the show with large artistic capitals—
I t's T hat M an A gain.   The title was, of course,
staring right at him.   When he said ITMA, we knew
our search was over. We just wondered why we hadn't
thought of it earlier.

Continuity with the earlier shows was vaguely maintained.   The broadcasting ship was scuppered at Scapa,

and Cilly was replaced by her sister Dotty. Vernon Harris ran the Guess or Know Feature. The Russian inventor changed his name from Vladivostooge to Vodkin. The rest of the details of that first war-time show, the first ITMA, belong to another chapter. For the time being it must suffice to say that the script was written, altered, revised, and re-written and sent away for duplicating. It came back stamped in red PROGRAMME CENSORED without a single word deleted or altered, and we were ready for the Air.

On the morning and afternoon of September 19th we rehearsed, and then at 9.30 that evening we went on the air from the Clifton Parish Hall before a small audience composed mainly of B.B.C. staff. Tommy was back once again in a " fit-up." A black-out system which would have delighted Heath Robinson had to be negotiated before one reached the oasis of light in this tiny building. There was a fanfare, the announcer gave the magic initials I.T.M.A., and the familiar signature tune by Michael North began. We were off on a ten year's run.

CHAPTER XI

BEFORE embarking on an account of the first year of ITMA and its subsequent success, it may be appropriate here to take stock of Tommy's position in the world of entertainment. At this time it appeared that he was at a standstill, and his first weeks in Bristol where, as a member of the Variety Rep., he had to take on any show whether it suited him or not, to use scripts which of necessity were hurriedly written, worried him considerably. Again, he was on the air day and night, a test which would have meant the end of some comedians, and yet he survived. ITMA was to raise him from the slough and to place him eventually on the highest pinnacle ever reached by a radio comedian.

Sharing digs with him, as I had shared his flat fourteen years previously, I was in a good position to study his reactions to Bristol and to the circumstances in which the war had placed him. Financially it meant a serious loss in income. It then appeared that music hall dates were a thing of the past, his contracts were now void, and his B.B.C. Repertory salary was, I believe, only about twenty-five pounds a week. Again, he was so much a home-loving man and a creature of habit who felt lost when his daily routine was upset, that Bristol irked him and he longed to escape. He was now about forty-five, extremely careful of his personal appearance, always with his tie matching his socks and with a neatly folded silk handkerchief harmonising with both. He drank little, not at all when he was working—played a little golf, rose early in the morning and rarely sat up late at night. He read a lot, usually biographies or crime fiction, never funny books or the works of leading humorists—and always he pined to get back to London.

A lot of his spare time was spent in Clifton Zoo. Rarely a day passed that he did not stroll round feeding the animals, fascinated by Alfred the enormous gorilla who got to know him quite well, distributing rubber bands to the smaller monkeys, who loved playing with them. On one young tigress he appeared to exert an almost hypnotic influence. The moment he appeared, she came to the bars, lay down, and stared fixedly at him. This happened so regularly that in time crowds used to follow him into the " cat " house just to see the performance. Had his voice the same effect on her as it had on his millions of listeners ? I never saw a smile on the face of the tiger, but I firmly believe that had he entered the cage, the tigress would have allowed him to stroke her and might even have sat up and begged. The Fellows at the Zoo suggested that on account of lack of visitors and shortage of food, animal lovers might like to help by adopting or sharing in the adoption of an animal. Tommy readily agreed, and so found himself the proud foster-father of half a camel— the other half being owned by a Bristol Girls' School. It was just his luck, he remarked, that *his* half was the one that had to be fed !

He soon became well known in the town, and was of course pursued by autograph hunters. Mr. W. L. Tracey, who was in charge of the evacuated B.B.C. staff at Bristol, tells me of a typical incident of those days. There was a pub near Whiteladies Road conveniently close to the B.B.C. headquarters. It became a sort of West Country Bolivar for broadcasting artistes —a fact soon discovered by the youngsters of the neighbourhood. In fact they became a bit of a nuisance, and the landlord, worried at the barrage of autograph books which were held under the noses of his patrons every time they appeared, used to shoo them off.

One day Tommy reversed the routine. He gently booted the landlord inside and followed him. The youngsters hung around for a while in the hopes that Tommy would re-emerge. He did, with the landlord carrying a tray of ginger-beers, which they drank, while Tommy scribbled his signature in their albums.

And so to the first performance of " It's That Man Again," in its new guise. Here was Tommy's opportunity of rehabilitation as a star radio man, and he seized it with both hands, as indeed did Francis Worsley and myself. Francis, although a highly experienced producer, had had little to do with either variety or comedy, and now had a free hand to exploit various theories that he held. I was also seeking a chance to try out ideas— I had by now been writing for radio, stage, screen and press for fifteen years, and yet was comparatively unknown—in fact in B.B.C. circles almost entirely unknown. It must be remembered that up till then radio writers had not come into their own. They received neither credit nor credits except in very few cases, and strange as it may seem, when the original Variety Repertory team had been formed, no provision for writers had been made with the exception of Max Kester, who was also a producer, Vernon Harris who had written much of Band Waggon—and was a producer also—and C. Denier Warren, who was included in the Rep. as

a performer. I was thus the first outside writer to be
co-opted, and this happened principally by the efforts
of Francis who was one of the first to realise that the
enormous war-time effort of the Variety Department
would necessitate the employment of not one but of
every available writer.

My own idea of radio-writing was an obvious one—
it was to use sound for all it was worth, the sound of
different voices and accents, the use of catch-phrases,
the impact of funny sounds in words, of grotesque
effects to give atmosphere—every device to create the
illusion of rather crazy or inverted reality.   In Francis
Worsley I found the ideal producer, unafraid of
innovations, helpful, receptive and unfailingly understanding. Tommy, too, got on well with him, admired
his breadth of judgment and knew instinctively that he
could put perfect trust in him. What was more, he
liked him.

We were then fortunate in our producer, and for ten
years we worked in perfect harmony. And yet in birth,
unbringing, education and political leanings no three
men could have been more different. There was Francis,
son of a Canon of the Church of England, born in the
shadow of the Cathedral, Public School, Oxford, the
Colonial Service, the B.B.C. Politically ? Well—let us
say he was a constant reader of the *New Statesman*.
Tommy—Liverpool, primary school, secondary school
up to the age of fifteen, toy salesman, chorus boy,
music hall, concert party, Savoy Hill—a Nonconformist,
politically tending towards Conservatism. Myself, a
Catholic, born in New Zealand, educated by the Marists,
medical student Edinburgh University and Barts, had
tried many things, none of them very successfully.
Politically, strong Labour leanings but definitely anti-

Socialist, a disciple of G. K. Chesterton—one of his first Distributists.

Of the three of us, Tommy had had the widest experience in entertainment. His comedy sense amounted to genius—he was the star, we were the stooges. If I have lingered unduly long on this description it is only because I think it important in as much as it affected ITMA and shaped Tommy's future. It proved too that three men differing so greatly in orientation could work amicably and in unison, and that in what must be one of the most nerve-racking occupations in the world— the constant effort to maintain a certain standard year after year—the responsibility for the entertainment of millions, especially during a World War—we neither quarrelled, sulked, struck, walked out or threw any kind of temperament. Would that nations could do the same !

In this amity Tommy, of course, played the principal part. He was never difficult ; he helped enormously once the script was written ; he could suggest the pointing of a gag, the re-writing of a line, which lifted it right out of the rut. He was gifted with an uncanny ear for the *sound* of words. He was generous in letting others get the laughs, unselfish, dependable, and unfailingly hard-working. No producer could wish for a better star—no writer could ever hope to receive such co-operation.

To put on record how ITMA came into being each week will dispel the idea that Tommy was a Worsley-Kavanagh puppet or alternatively that he simply had to get in front of a microphone and start talking to be a success. ITMA was thrashed out by many hours of brain-teasing labour by the three of us sitting round one desk. My preliminary script had been typed in triplicate, and we read it over slowly. Tommy would read aloud a sentence or two, savouring the style and testing for accentuation. Most broadcasters doodle all over their scripts with their own private hieroglyphics, which mean " raise the voice," " pause," and so on. Tommy very rarely did this. He had a photographic, or rather phonographic, memory. These miniature rehearsals of his caused a lot of revision of the script. Sentences would be switched, different words chosen. We would go over it again and again.

Tommy had the innate sense of the born comedian to the audience's reaction. Although the studio patrons were but a tiny section of the unseen millions who were listening to him, he was always able to sum up exactly which sequence went well, and which went badly. We used to have an inquest next day after we heard the play-back. Tommy was always there, and both Francis and I relied implicitly on his views as to which had been the most successful lines. As I had to write the following week's show over the week-end immediately after the Thursday broadcast, there was no chance of relying on listeners' letters or the B.B.C. listener research section for information. But it wasn't necessary. Tommy's opinion always proved absolutely reliable. This was not only useful for outlining the general plan of the subsequent show ; once my script was delivered he was able to read over the dialogue (imitating any of the characters to give a perfect one-man show), and thus give us a very good idea of what should be kept in and what should go out. A goodish slice always went out, and then I would start writing new material to replace it.

For the statistically minded it may be news to know that the actual dialogue of ITMA occupied an average of eighteen and a half minutes out of the half-hour show, and in this time we tried for at least one hundred potential laughs. Sometimes there were more. I don't say that any one listener chortled one hundred times. If there was such a person he wouldn't have been able to hear all the dialogue anyway. But it is a fact that many people who listened to the repeat broadcasts wrote and told us that they had made the second session —the repeat—a habit because a line, which did not raise even the vestige of a smile on Thursday seemed funny on Sunday, and, as Norman the Doorman would have said, " vikky-verky." There were, as I have explained, supposed to be one hundred gags—or one every eleven seconds to give someone somewhere his quota of amusement. If we reduced it to ninety because we couldn't cudgel our brains for the other ten, several million people would say that " ITMA wasn't as good as last week," and they would have been right. On the other hand, if we got a laugh every eight seconds, as sometimes we did, then the show was regarded as a smasher !

Added to this problem, there was the necessity to include all the characters and all their lines. I always kept a list of their names in front of me when writing the script, and ticked off each one as he or she appeared. I *did* try to be fair ! Tommy always said that the principal characteristic of listeners was intense loyalty. A tremendous sense of disappointment was felt when a character was dropped, or when he or she failed to make his usual quota of wisecracks. Mrs. Mopp could not come in merely with her " Can I do you now, sir ? " and a request to dust the dado ; she had to bring a present ; she had to be slightly bawdy ; and she had to fade out with initialled adieus. To the very end people were writing in to ask that Funf should come back when there was no reason to have a German spy lurking about the place even in a show as crazy at ITMA ; and every one of the scores of characters portrayed by the versatile Jack Train caused nostalgic memories among people who had remembered them from the early war years.

On the face of it it would have appeared that these characters, let loose before the microphone, would give us all the laughs we needed. But they would have failed utterly without the pivot round which they all whirled. Tommy rarely left the microphone for the entire half-hour of the show, bluffing his way out of awkward situations, suave, seriously light-hearted, allowing others to score off him, distributing the laughter equally between himself and his opposite number—a style of patter which broke every convention of the old-time music hall and of the younger radio comedy technique. Most people know that the majority of variety acts can be analysed as " comic and feed," " wisecracker and stooge." Tommy was neither—yet both. If Funf fed him with comedy opportunities one minute, Tommy fed Mrs. Mopp with them the next. It was tremendously hard work for Tommy to switch from one to the other a score of times in every show, and is one of the many reasons why ITMA died with him.

CHAPTER XII

THE FIRST ITMA

THE first ITMA show had a very big listening audience, for the closing of cinemas and theatres and the black-out difficulties meant that the radio programmes were the principal form of recreation in the evenings. This was undoubtedly one reason why it seemed to leap into national prominence from that first broadcast. Another was the infectious cheeriness of Tommy's voice, a voice they knew, which brought a real zest into a life beset with the troubles of children's evacuation to the country, husbands and sons disappearing into the services, and the huge mass of orders flowing from Authority to every one of forty-eight million people.

As a matter of fact, many of the characters which were later to become so famous did not appear in that first series, and there were not many catch phrases. After Tommy introduced himself as ITMA (" No, not ITLA ") Vera Lennox made her début as Dotty, the secretary ; Billy Ternent and his band proved that they had obeyed the order to place themselves entirely at the service of the Ministry ; Jack Train, in the guise of Fusspot, assistant controller, complained that everything was " most irregular, most irregular " ; Inventor Vodkin (Maurice Denham) arrived from the Ministry of Mis-Construction to work in any capacity, and demonstrated his spy detector ; Tommy enjoyed himself very much with all of them.

Reading the script of that first broadcast indicates many things. One is that ITMA developed gradually into a far slicker show during its long run. Another is that this programme could clearly never have been made a success by just anybody. Read as an ordinary piece of literature it is not, by the most generous standards, particularly funny. Innumerable people who tried to analyse ITMA's appeal suggested that the whole value was in the script ; they were wrong. Just as many said that Tommy's crackerjack voice made something very big out of something very small or nonexistent ; they were also wrong. A few discerning ones suggested that production had the key to success. They were also wide of the target. In retrospect it is easy to see that all three factors were essential. None could succeed by itself. By good luck, personal desire, and a lot of hard work three people had found a plan in which they could all do just what they wanted to do

But it would be absurd to ignore the fact that Tommy was the be-all and end-all of ITMA once it went on the air. On analysis, he probably spoke for less than ten minutes in any half-hour show. He appeared in innumerable fantastic guises, yet was essentially Tommy Handley all the time. The listener might picture in his mind's eye a Minister at a large desk, a Mayor of a seaside resort, a Governor of a colony, and so on ; but the disguise was very thin. One immediately visualised the familiar Tommy with an obviously glued-on moustache, or some sort of uniform which barely concealed his workaday suit underneath. In contrast, the characters who beset every minute of his career were always complete impersonations. One actor often played several parts. To the listener they were different people who had always had their quaint peculiarities and voices or vices. Tommy sat astride a world of peculiar people. He was the only ordinary person among a mass of " real characters," and yet he seemed to be the craziest of them all. There will be little criticism of my belief that no one else could possibly have portrayed this contradiction of terms as he did.

There is one other feature of ITMA which will be understandable only to people of extremely good memories. I myself cannot now understand some of the jokes. They were skits on a nine hours' wonder—a headline of that day's paper, and dead the following week. But if these individual cracks of Tommy's have lost their point by now, there is still the fact that every programme is an accurate reflection of the war situation at the time.

In reading the script of the first ITMA of September, 1939, one savours it better if one recalls the trend of events at that period. Total war had not materialised. The first hectic days of upheaval had quietened a little. People were floundering about in the black-out in the darker evenings of autumn. Civil defence officials were busy seeing that people had cleared their lofts and built shelters in the garden. Millions of leaflets on passive defence, food storage, rationing and gas poured through the nation's letter-boxes. In France the Maginot line stood impregnable, and the Siegfried Line was becoming a joke. It was a funny sort of war, and the principal annoyances seemed to come from the authorities who wanted to poke their noses into everyone's affairs. Behind the sticky tape on the windows the nation kept its gas masks handy and rather wondered what it was all about.

ITMA was ready to explain.

Here is the first ITMA script, broadcast on Tuesday, September 19th, 1939 :

TOMMY (*with Band*) : It's that man again,
     Yes, that man again,
     Yes, sir, Tommy Handley is here.

ANNOUNCER (*over Music*) : A radio show with Vera
    Lennox, Jack Train, Maurice Denham, Sam
    Costa, Jack Hylton's Band, conducted by
    Billy Ternent, and Tommy Handley.

VERA : Mother's pride and joy,
    Mrs. Handley's boy,
    Oh, it's useless to complain
    When trouble's brewing, it's his doing,
    That man—that man again.

TOMMY : Heil, folks—it's Mein Kampf again—sorry, I
    should say hello folks, it's that man again.
    That was a Goebbled version—a bit doctored.
    I usually go all goosey when I can't follow
    my proper-gander. That broadcasting ship
    of mine was commandeered and scuppered at
    Scapa and I've been taken over by the Govern-
    ment. Yes, they've made me Minister of
    Aggravation and Mysteries and put me in
    charge of the Office of Twerps, otherwise
    known as ITMA.

     (*'Phone rings.*)

TOMMY : Hello—yes—this is ITMA. ITMA—no, not
    ITLA—ITMA ! (*Sings*) Itma, itma, mi—mi
    —mi—mi. What's ITMA ? I.T.M.A.—*It*'s
    *T*hat *M*an *A*gain. No—sorry, the pigeon post
    is late to-day, the postman ate the express
    messenger—feathers and all. I haven't had a
    word from any of my spies. When I get
    these spies here I won't mince my words,
    I can tell you. Ring me up again when
    I'm out. Good-bye, or, as they say in
    Pomerania, 'arf window screen. Now where's
    my new secretary ?

VERA : Here I am, Mr. Handtorch.

TOMMY : Well, puncture me with a portfolio. Are you my new secretary?

VERA : Yes. I'm Dotty.

TOMMY : I'm balmy myself. My last secretary was Cilly and you're Dotty.

VERA : Cilly was my sister.

TOMMY : Well, splash my spats! Cilly was your sister? I'll have to see a silly-sister—a lawyer —about this.

VERA : My brother's potty.

TOMMY : Nice family. What drove your brother into the giggle house?

VERA : Oh, they drove him in a taxi.

TOMMY : No, no—what caused his mental aberration?

VERA : He didn't have an operation. He thought he was a sundial.

TOMMY : And found he couldn't wind himself up?

VERA : No; for ten years he went out every morning at sunrise and turned slowly round from east to west.

TOMMY : But a sundial doesn't turn round.

VERA : I know. And when I told him that, he just went scatty.

TOMMY : You're as silly as your sister.

VERA : Oh, Mr. Handlebar, I think I'm going to get on with you.

TOMMY : Well, don't try and get off with me. And my name is Handley—there's an accent on the " ley " and nothing on the hand. Can you answer the 'phone?

VERA : It hasn't spoken to me yet.

TOMMY : I suppose you can type?

VERA : Oh yes, I'm a touch typist.

TOMMY : Don't try and touch me for anything. Take a memo. : " To all concerned in the Office of Twerps : Take notice that from to-day, September the twenty-tooth, I, the Minister of

Aggravation, have power to confiscate, complicate and commandeer . . ."

VERA : How do you spell commandeer, Mr. Hanwell?

TOMMY : Commandeer—let me see. (*Sings*) Comm-om-and-eer, comm-on-and-eer, Tommy Handley's wag-time band, comm-on-and-eer, etc. . . . Er, where were we? " I have the power to seize anything on sight."

VERA : Oh, Mr. Handpump—and me sitting so close to you!

TOMMY : Keep your mind on your memo. " From to-day onwards Jack Hylton's band is placed entirely at the service of this Ministry, for work of the utmost national annoyance, and all sufferers from syncopation must report immediately to me, when they will receive a first fiddle copy of the Warden's Farewell to his Whistle. Signed T.H., on behalf of ITMA."

VERA : What sort of paper shall I type it on?

TOMMY : Soft. Now, send in my assistant controller. What's his name?

VERA : You mean Mr. Fusspot.

TOMMY : Fusspot? Well, butter my bath-bun, is that a name or a utensil?

VERA : Oh, it's his name. He's been here since the days when this was the Office of Squirts. If you press that bell on your desk nothing will happen, but if you shout up the chimney Mr. Fusspot will come down.

TOMMY : That'll suit me all right. And if I hang up my stocking he'll creep in and fill it full of restrictions, I suppose. Send him in at once.
(*'Phone rings.*)
Yes, this is ITMA. What? You want to take over Peabody's Buildings, to use as Headquarters for the Ministry of Mothballs.

Certainly, take over the whole place immediately. Chuck everybody out. Move in at once. And I say, send a few along to me; I've got moths in my main-spring.

(*Knock at door.*)

FUSSPOT : Er, you sent for me? I'm Mr. Fusspot, assistant controller.

TOMMY : I wish you'd control your moustache. You'll never get a gas-mask on over that.

FUSSPOT : This is most irregular, most irregular.

TOMMY : Irregular—it's like a beer-stained haystack. Why don't you trim it?

FUSSPOT : You are sending out orders, sir, in all directions, without reference to me. Yesterday you sent five hundred aeroplanes over England distributing football coupons. You are issuing ration cards with pictures of Teddy Brown on them. It's most irregular, most irregular.

TOMMY : Listen to me, Fusspot, my job is to bring everyone up to scratch by irritating them as much as I can. When I can't think of anything more diabolical, I'll get the band to play. I'm broadcasting to the whole of Britain in ten minutes' time to tell everyone what to expect from the Office of Twerps, so you get back to your dug-out; and another thing, next time you make tea in your tin-hat—turn over a new leaf.

FUSSPOT : It's most irregular, most irregular.

(*'Phone rings.*)

TOMMY : Hullo, ITMA speaking. Hitler signed a pact with a man in the moon; ah, well, the higher the Fuehrer. Well, I'll be confiscated, here's my entertainment manager, Vernon Harris, specially engaged for amusement only. Have you got Jack Hylton's band here?—as if I didn't know.

VERNON : Tes, Tommy.

TOMMY : Don't forget their numbers are strictly rationed to-night. Tell 'em not to play too loud, my foot's asleep.

VERNON : All right, tell it to wake up and dream. That brings us to Jack Hylton's band, who have been fast asleep for the last five minutes. They are waking up now, moistening their lips, smiling pleasantly, and getting ready to play a warmed-up version of " Tea for Two." What you might call a third cup !

(Band play : " Tea for Two.")

TOMMY : Bill Ternent, take the boys out and liquidate them and save one for me.

FUSSPOT : Here I am, sir. This music in a Government office is most irregular.

TOMMY : Well have it banned. That was the conductor's fault.

FUSSPOT : The conductor ?

TOMMY : Yes. Jack Hylton's left-ternant. I'll get all the names in if it kills me.

FUSSPOT : This office, sir, is being turned into a Bedlam.

TOMMY : Yes, it's full of sheet music. What's the matter ?

FUSSPOT : Ten million mousetraps have just arrived. Did you order them ?

TOMMY : Of course I did. Put 'em in the band room. I want to get rid of the maestro.

FUSSPOT : And who cancelled the black-out to-night ?

TOMMY : I did. I'm going to darken every town in the daytime and light it up at night. That'll fool 'em.

FUSSPOT : It's most irregular, most irregular.

TOMMY : Fusspot, do me a favour. Take out your pocket knife and cut me a caper.

FUSSPOT : But you must sign me an order, sir.

TOMMY : What's this ? Order for the prohibition of

peanuts in public places. I'll sign everything that prohibits anything. That's what I'm here for. Get fifty million pamphlets printed.

FUSSPOT : Fifty million pamphlets, sir ?

TOMMY : Yes, cancelling all the pamphlets issued already. And 'phone the B.B.C. and tell 'em I've got so thin I'm coming along to join the skeleton staff. Finally, if anyone is doing anything, tell 'em to stop it at once. And put a notice on the door saying " Business as usual during altercations."

VERA : Mr. Handbasin . . .

TOMMY : Well, kiss me in the control room ! What'll you call me next ? We've got a Fusspot and you call me handbasin. We'll have the whole set in a minute. Bring me a cup of tea and some sandwiches.

VERA : What kind of sandwiches ?

TOMMY : Achtung.

VERA : Oh, I forgot to tell you, there's a gentleman waiting to see you in a hurry.

TOMMY : He'll never see me in a hurry. This is a Government office.

VERA : He's brought his baggage with him.

TOMMY : His baggage ? Tell him to wait outside and send her in. Fusspot, make out an order to prohibit water from running under bridges and . . . well, pluck my eyebrows with a pick-axe, look what's blown in. Who are you ?

VODKIN : My name is Vodkin.

TOMMY : My mother used to use one of your family to pull the cord through the top of my pyjamas.

VODKIN : No, I am plain Vodkin.

TOMMY : I must knock you back some time. What's your nationality if any ?

VODKIN : I am neuter.

TOMMY : Neuter ? What's on your agenda ?

VODKIN : My wife. She was Bavarian.

TOMMY : And where if your old Deutch now ?

VODKIN : She is now an interrupter.

TOMMY : So's mine. I can't get a word in edgeways.

VODKIN : I am sent by the Ministry of Mis-construction to offer myself in any incapacity.

TOMMY : You've come to the right place. ITMA'S full of incapacity. Can you cook ?

VODKIN : I can cook, so.

TOMMY : Sew ? Then you can sew a button on my pants. It's getting a bit late in the year to wear open-neck trousers.

VODKIN : No. I Vodkin, am a great technical expert.

TOMMY : Well, all I can say is you're a very odd Vodkin.

VODKIN : You need me, Mr. Handley. Tell me, what is the function of your Office of Twerps ?

TOMMY : I haven't the slightest idea. It is so secret that I don't even allow myself to tell myself anything. The place is full of spies. I'm one myself.

VODKIN : Spies—ah, I have in my bag a spy detector. See, I conceal myself beneath the carpet, so ? It is invisible, yes ?

TOMMY : No. What happens if a spy enters the room ?

VODKIN : A bell rings all over the building.

TOMMY (*sings*) : " Loudly the bell in the old tower rings." All right, Vodkin. I'll try anything once. I'll hand you over to my assistant, Mr. Fusspot. (*Calls*) Fusspot, forward !

FUSSPOT : Really, Mr. Handley, this is most irreg——
           (*Bells ring in all directions.*)

VODKIN : Ah, a spy. See my doctor detector has already proved itself. Shall I shoot him now ?

TOMMY : No, go and shoot the door. You've been leaning against the bell push.
           (*Bedlam of bells.*)

VERNON : Oh, that'll do, you're give me Bells in the
Batfry. In any case lay off, for here comes
Sam Costa and Jack Hylton's band in a new
number, " Moon Love."
(Band plays " Moon Love.")

FUSSPOT : Mr. Handley, Mr. Handley, here is a letter
it's marked urgent.

TOMMY : Urgent? Oh, it's probably from the Office
of Internal Disintegration. Throw it away.

FUSSPOT : Most irregular, sir. Please, please, it is also
marked Priority.

TOMMY : I haven't time for toothpaste adverts.

VODKIN : But, Mr. Handley, it also says Secret.

TOMMY : Well, in that case I can't read it, can I?

VODKIN : Mr. Handley, it's very important. It comes
from the Censor's Office.

TOMMY : Then it's out—anyway, give it to me. Hay,
wait a minute, folks, this is big stuff; it's
colossal, get a load of this. Listen !
(Follows " Sing a Song of the Censor.")
*(At this stage there came the Guess or No
feature and a special spot for Tommy Handley so that he could explain his Ministry's
plans. The show then resumes.)*

VERA : Oh, Mr. Handley, this is awful. I was sitting
in my office and two men came in and pinched
my seat.

TOMMY : Prove it.

FUSSPOT : Oh, this is most irregular, most irregular.
This entire building has been taken over.
We all have to leave immediately.

VERA : This is an outrage. They have removed my
bags.

TOMMY : Just a Japanese Sandman. What's all this?
I didn't give an order to confiscate this building? I said they could take Peabody Buildings.

ALL : This is Peabody Buildings.

Tommy : Well, prod me with a pantechnicon. We are
turned out of our own offices. Never mind,
folks, the Office of Twerps will carry on ;
next week we'll annoy you once again.

Next week they duly did. The Minister had by then
found accommodation in Blotto's Brewery, where ITMA
proposed to stay for bitter or worse. This programme
introduced one of the most famous characters of the
series—Funf. He was the embodiment of every spy,
the crystallisation of every enemy agent story retailed
in their hundreds by people up and down the country.
His name was created quite accidentally. Francis
Worsley's small son was proud of his ability to count
in German—his teacher being an Austrian woman
refugee, a Doctor of Law from Vienna, who was living
in the Worsley home at the time. Worsley came back
tired from a conference with Tommy and myself at
which we had been trying to find a name for the spy
whose activities were already written in rough outline.
Master Worsley started quite well : " *Ein, zwei, drei,
vier, funf.*" There he stuck. His father suddenly realised
that the perfect name was discovered.

The ubiquitous spy's " This is Funf speaking " was
the big gag used by the public in general that winter.
His name debunked every hair-raising spy story. Children played games based on M.I.5 and Funf. The
insidious German secret service machine was reduced to
a music hall—or rather, radio—joke.

Funf's first 'phone call came at the beginning of this
second programme. His message shook Tommy considerably, and he arranged for Fusspot to get him a
life insurance policy for nine million marks.

The programme also had a feature called " Interned
To-night," from the secret camp of Popple Cowhide,

Berks. This was the time when large numbers of people were being sent to the Isle of Man, and the internment of enemy aliens was in everybody's mind. Like most of those people in actuality, the internees who came to the microphone were rather harmless characters : Herr Schnitzel, the waiter ; Herr Cutt, a West End barber.

Considerable excitement was caused when an invention revealed that Dotty was in fact Sonia Sourpuss, a beautiful spy who kept codes in her corsage and documents in her *déshabillé*. And more than that, under hypnosis, she revealed that her master was none other than Tommy himself.

In the third edition these minor problems were conveniently forgotten with the general terror of Funf's activities and the arrival of a woman spy—Helga Schwenk. Her name, by the way, was given after a censor's rejection of the original one. She was a seductive woman, and her perfume had the desired effect on Tommy, who gave her several drawersful of plans.

In the fourth programme Maurice Denham played a new character—Mrs. Tickle, the charwoman. Although Funf warned Tommy that she was a spy, Lola Tickle was a charming old girl, who proudly boasted that " she always did her best for all her gentlemen." She was different from the Mrs. Mopp of later programmes —more sprightly. As she said to Tommy, she was always one for a lark.

At the time of this broadcast the " Guess or No " feature was replaced by a burlesque of a Continental commercial show. A very large number of people used to listen to Radio Luxembourg in pre-war days, but these programmes abruptly ceased when war broke out. ITMA filled the gap with Radio Fakenburg, the

programme opening with the announcer's warning :
" Mesdames et Messieurs, Defense de Cracher." Costa
sang the commercial and Tommy gave the spot announcements on behalf of the ITMA car—" A square deal and
a square wheel."

By November the show was running very smoothly,
even though Tommy's activities in it gave him a stormy
passage. The Government tried to close his Ministry ;
crowds stood outside and shouted " Down with ITMA,"
and the camouflage unit made everyone invisible—so
invisible indeed that Tommy could not find his own
desk. On November 21st, Sam Costa stepped out of
the band and played the part of Lemuel, Vodkin's
adenoidal lab. boy. He hadn't the slightest idea of
the fame in store for him in later years.

Then the Office of Twerps was evacuated. In the
hide-out " somewhere in England " there were a number
of truly rural characters, including Farmer Jollop,
played by Jack Train. At this stage another ITMA
catch phrase made its début. It was a senseless one in
which any remark ending with the word " Friday," or
a word with a similar sound, brought the retort " Friday ? " and the counter-retort " Friday ! " It got so
that no one dared mention the word because of the
inevitable sequence of replies. Another perfect *non
sequitur* which Tommy inserted into his dialogue and
found people repeating all over the place was " I wish
I had as many shillings." This had been a favourite
saying of a great comedian, Jimmy Learmouth, who
Tommy worshipped in his youth.

The series ended on February 6th, 1940. The Office
of Twerps' country residence had been commandeered
by the army ; Tommy had packed everyone into cara-
vans, and as he sung in the words of the big hit of the

war, and later to be Vera Lynn's signature tune, " We'll Meet Again—don't know where, don't know when . . ." the cavalcade set off to find a new home and also to find Funf.

It had been a very successful season. War-time broadcasting was now running smoothly, and apart from the difficulties of working from billets and make-shift studios in Bristol, there were no complaints—not even from the Censors. Looking over the scripts of that 1939-40 series, I see that only two alterations were made by the Censor—one on the lady spy's name and one in mid-January, when Tommy said that there was a frost outside. People who remember struggling with burst pipes and icy roads in that first war winter will agree that there certainly was—but it was then a State secret.

CHAPTER XIII

ITMA LEAVES THE AIR

OVER a year was to elapse before Tommy was heard on the air again. Indeed, it was almost seventeen months later that ITMA returned—this time in Bangor, North Wales. Its sudden departure in February, 1940, was—in some ways—the penalty of its success. Here was the old Handley, the favourite of fifteen years, back again at the top of his form—in fact a new Handley—it was " That Man," revived, rejuvenated, streaking ahead of all competition, cheering those who were worried and depressed by the war. A sure sign of his success was the inclusion in every Christmas pantomime of his sayings and slogans. There was hardly a panto throughout Britain which didn't have Funf in it or a dame who, Tickle-fashion, didn't do her best for " all her gentlemen."

To that astute showman, Jack Hylton—Tommy's old partner—this appeared to be the opportune moment to produce a stage version. He had already bought the Stage and Film rights, so in February I found myself committed to re-write ITMA for the stage at only a few days' notice. Jack spared nothing, neither time nor money—the show was due to open in less than a fortnight, Robert Nesbitt was engaged to produce it—and a very elaborate production it was. It was always a pleasure to work with Jack Hylton—I had written the scripts for his " Youth Takes a Bow " and " Playtime " before the war—I enjoyed his company and admired his instinctive showmanship. He was always quiet and understanding, and there was something about him which inspired a writer as all will agree who have worked with him. But you had to work; he was untiring himself—a hard task-master with a kind heart. Tommy, too, was one of his greatest admirers: after all, both members of the short-lived double act, " Hylton and Handley," had gone right to the top—and success had not changed them.

They both enjoyed a parody of the Flotsam and Jetsam signature tune I had written for Jack's " Playtime," and both sang it with what is known as " gusto."

BOTH : We'll tell you our names, and we'll tell them quite blandly.
TOM : I'm Handley.
JACK : I'm Hylton.
JACK : I'm Hylton.
TOM : I'm Handley.
JACK : Now I'm a big cheese.
TOM : A regular Stilton.
JACK : I'm Hylton.
TOM : I'm Handley.
TOM : Tom Handley.
JACK : Jack Hylton.
BOTH : These are the names that our fame has been built on.
TOM : You ought to see Hylton when he's got his kilt on.
JACK : Tommy can't wear one—his legs are too bandly.
BOTH : Yours very sincerely, Hylton and Handley.

Naturally there were other versions ! We rehearsed the new show day and night for a week, and after a twenty-hour rehearsal on the Sunday and Monday prior to production, ITMA opened at the Hippodrome, Birmingham, on February 29th—a little over a fortnight after the last broadcast in Bristol.

The stage production followed the radio version. Maurice Denham, waiting to be called up, played Mrs. Tickle, and Jack Train was Funf, Farmer Jollop, and other characters. Johnny Lockwood took Sam Costa's place, June Malo supplied the glamour, and Billy Cotton's band the music. There was a chorus of sixteen, a performing horse, and many additions to the original broadcasting team. The opening scene was set outside the Ministry of Aggravation where a shower of pamphlets heralded the arrival of Tommy by parachute. Funf 'phoned from a convenient kiosk. Mrs. Tickle answered, and the show began. To make the parachute descent, Tommy had to wear harness—a kind of straight jacket, corset affair with a wire attached ; he was strung up and suspended in the " flies " five minutes before the curtain rose. He hated it—he always swore it had altered his voice ! His discomfort was no less easy to bear when, he saw, his wire-man calmly tied him up and walked away until it was time to be lowered on to the stage.

On the first night the hook which Tommy had detached when he landed got caught in the scenery and remained there during Tommy's opening lines, but mishaps like this are common on opening nights and the production, despite the rush, went smoothly on. A six months' tour followed—but after Birmingham the parachute descent was abolished and Tommy, the ex-R.N.A.S. balloon expert, entered his Office of Twerps on a scooter. Now, although packed houses greeted the show everywhere, the tour could hardly have been called a success. It was an expensive production ; it had colour, glamour

E

and expert direction—but it just was not funny. In short, it was impossible to transfer the radio version which, for its success, depended on sound alone, to the stage. In other words, the ITMA characters, unlike good children, were designed to be heard and not seen. As far as Tommy was concerned, the difference between his stage and radio personality was very obvious—he did not appear to be the cheery carefree man of Itma and his unerring instinct told him that the stage version was wrong.

The tour went on into a second—rather reduced—edition, in which Tommy resurrected the ever-green "Disorderly Room." By this time Hitler had over-run Europe, the Battle of Britain had been fought and won, the Blitz had started, and although the tour continued and Tommy performed during many a "hot" night of bombs and incendiaries in the suburban halls round London, one by one they closed and the stage version of ITMA ended for all time. From now onwards Tommy was to spend almost all his time in London with Jean, either at their flat in Bayswater, or at their cottage at Egham. Here Jean and her mother had together designed a beautiful garden, and it was one of Tommy's greatest joys to spend his few free hours pottering, relaxing on the lawn or tutoring "Laura" the parrot, who knew his voice so well that she laughed loudly whenever she heard it coming out of the loud-speaker. The rest of his time was spent between his weekly visits to Bangor and at the Criterion Theatre for "Handley's Half Hour," which reached a total of one hundred consecutive broadcasts.

The end of the ITMA tour coincided with another move of the B.B.C. headquarters. Raids on the West of England aimed at—and missing—the great aircraft works at Filton had caused damage to many of the makeshift studios at Bristol, which was badly blitzed. On more than one occasion a programme had to be faded out because of the noise of bombs and gunfire. In February, 1941, came the order to move to Bangor. A special train took officials, engineers and artistes to the no-man's-land of North Wales, as it then seemed. I had been sent on in advance just before Christmas, and I must admit I hated it. A series I was writing was singularly unsuccessful, my billet was incredibly uncomfortable, I had lost all I ever possessed in London, I had been badly battered by the blitz in Bristol, the Bangor folk were strange and not very friendly ; I felt that depression could not descend to greater depths. My great refuge in despair was Michael North, then in charge of B.B.C. Variety at Bangor (now producing Music Hall), and many a pint we sank together in the snug of a pub where we could get away from it all. His position was not a very comfortable one, but he survived it all and—like me—breathed a sigh of relief when the special train bearing the whole weight of the Variety Department arrived.

The arrival of this cavalcade of Variety brought a degree of terror into the hearts of some of the citizens of Bangor. " What ? " said one of these—" our High Street filled with painted women and acrobats ! " Gradually, however, they got used to it—parish halls, hotels and offices were commandeered, canteens established, a theatre taken over, a colony and club set up on the near-by Island of Anglesey, people flocked in and money poured in. Soon the fears of the Bangorians were stilled. Later, they took us all to their warm Welsh hearts and as a plaque presented to the B.B.C. testifies, they were sorry when three years later the Variety

Department returned to London—lock, stock and microphone.

My relief when Francis Worsley arrived may be imagined. I've rarely been so pleased to see anyone. Now we could start ITMA again, and my joy was re-doubled when Tommy came down from London for a preliminary conference. He had a soft spot for North Wales, where he had spent many a holiday in his school-days, and he was delighted to renew acquaintance with the haunts of his youth. He made great play with Welsh place-names—Twyr Gwyn Chapel Hall, where Francis had his office, reminded him of the old music hall favourite—Chirgwin, the White-Eyed Kaffir, and so became Twyr Gwyn the White-Eyed Chapel. He was delighted to find that his telephone exchange was TWYNY GONGEL—nothing could have been more appropriate.

I had thought a lot about ITMA while I was isolated (or interned) in Bangor, and had dotted down a lot of new characters and ideas which, when presented to Francis, were at once accepted. Thus, Lefty and Sam (the gentle gangsters), the Diver, the Colonel, Ali Oop (the pedlar), the cheery Commercial Traveller, Claude and Cecil (the polite brokers' men), and many others were born.

Francis had now moved his office to the High Street, and there we three gathered round a table to compare notes and to line up the next show.

We realised right away that cracks, however kindly, at Government Departments would no longer be appro-priate. The country was now fighting for its life and still expecting invasion. People had all the war news they wanted, and even the mock-activities of the ITMA Ministry might seem a little wearying to a people who

Every penny makes the water warmer." There was a diver's helmet on the ground and the man wore a bathing suit, but despite long waits in the area by a hopeful Tommy, he never saw him put even his toe in the water. There was also a one-legged diver who really *did* dive.

Tommy's appreciation of this gentleman's remarks paid a huge dividend in popularity. It was the easiest of all the catch phrases of the series to imitate. Fighter pilots on the " Circuses " which were by that time prodding into enemy-held territory across the Channel shouted it over the inter-com. as they dived to shoot up ground targets : " I'm going down now, sir "—sometimes the last words they ever spoke. Children annoyed their teachers with it in hushed moments in class, and no lift attendant worthy of the name—from the men in the mines to the ageing ladies who had replaced the svelte beauties in the department stores—used any other phrase as they carried out their duties.

Sam Scram also brought along his gangster pal, Lefty, who had none of the respect for Tommy shown by Sam. His first comment on the Mayor-elect was :

" He's a big palooka—get out your gat and shoot up this joint." Fortunately Lefty always missed. This show also presented one of the film interludes which became so popular. The first one was introduced :

" Fog Bound Films Inc. present an all-coughing, all-sneezing, all-spluttering epic photographed in glorious khaki colour entitled ' Tom Marches ON ' . . ." Needless to say, with gangster methods and a little vote-fiddling Tommy won the election easily. " Well, nip me in the nosebag " was his comment and only address to his supporters when the figures were announced.

In the following week's show His Washout the Mayor

discussed his coat-of-arms—" Handley rompant with two beauty queens recumbent." New characters came along. Frau Funf, for instance, and Nimrod Nark, town clerk and borough treasurer. Jack Train added this rôle to his rapidly growing repertoire. It was in his first chat with this ancient worthy (he'd been with the Corporation for seventy years come Pontefract) that a preliminary taste of the " initial " gag was used. It went like this :

TOMMY : Er—as a reward for your faithful service I hereby confer on you the B.T.M.
JACK : What's that, your Worship ?
TOMMY : The Boro' Treasurer Medal.

The third show brought two famous characters to the show—Claude and Cecil. Jack Train and Horace Percival played these rôles, and their first introduction to radio audiences came when they entered the " Mer's " parlour to lay the " lilloleum." The preliminary dialogue was simple. It went like this :

HORACE : By your leave, sir.
JACK : After you, Claude——
HORACE : No, after you, Cecil.
TOMMY : I'll be after you both in a minute—what are you doing here ?
JACK : We've come to lay the lilloleum.
TOMMY : Lay the lilloleum ? Who ordered lilloleum ?
HORACE : No one. Move your chair, Mister. To *you*, Cecil.
JACK : No—to *YOU*, Claude.
TOMMY : Get out of here and take your lilloleum with you.
JACK : Right. After *you*, Claude.
HORACE : No—after *you*, Cecil.

It seems almost a natural conversation in cold print. At rehearsal it frankly did not sound so remarkably funny. But by the end of the show we knew, from the audience's amusement, that Cecil and Claude would have to come along next week and for many weeks—indeed years—after that.

This show as broadcast on America's Independence Day, and the musical interlude serenaded the democracy which was giving Britain " all aid short of war " with a special arrangement of " Yankee Doodle." There was another little topical touch in the Funf 'phone conversation. The spy complained that all his peace offers had been spurned. This was a reference to the rumoured offers of the laurel branch coming from Germany at the time.

The fourth programme marked the début of Hari Kari, the Japanese Sandman. He conducted telephone conversations with Tommy which were complete gibberish, though Tommy's replies permitted those who wished to fit on their own construction to the conversation. The first one drew the advice from Tommy : " You'll find it at the end of the pier." Ten minutes later, in response to anxious Japanese enquiries, Tom said : " Haven't you found it yet ? It was there last week." To the audience Tommy explained that his Nipponese friend was unable to locate the Post Office.

Whether this was quite true or not became doubtful in the next show when Hari was told " It's closed for repairs." Even in the last of the series the difficulty had not been solved, to Tommy's mystification, for, as he said : " I know it's open. I went there myself yesterday."

The finale brought some unusual gestures of friendship from Funf. Tommy treated these as the nation treated the real-life overtures of Funf's Führer. The arch spy's wily offering was stated in a letter which Tommy read aloud : " All I have said back I will take. All I have done I will undo. Your buddy I want to be. Peace we will make. Meet me at the lighthouse at 8.45 to-night—double crossing time." Everyone went along to surround Funf. Tommy actually saw him through the keyhole. But, of course, he escaped as usual.

The second series of shows ended with a promise from Tommy that he would be resuming his Mayoral Seat at the end of September, and the music faded with the company promising " ITSA—ITSA—ITSA date ! "

It had been a very short but exciting season. When Tommy met us on the following day for an inquest I think we all realised that it was a case of " ITMA is dead—long live ITMA." We agreed that the series deserved at least another airing as soon as possible, but cock-a-hoop as we were I don't think any of us on that July morning in 1941 would have believed that there would be similar pow-wows at intervals for another seven years.

Tommy went off with his wife for a few days to see his mother who still lived in the old home outside Liverpool. He could now tell the lady, who was always his severest and most stimulating critic, that the idea he had had in 1915 to get on the stage and leave commerce had been a good one.

Well known as he had been for many years, the rise to what was now, literally, national fame was remarkable. Basically, the traditional ITMA programme had not arrived until this 1941 series of " It's That Sand Again." In this the old ideas of " Guess or No," and so on, had gone. The cast, coming in and out of the ITMA door, the special musical arrangements, the characters with their catch-phrase trade marks, the whole set-up was there for the first time.

Before we separated for a brief break we roughed out the theme for the next series. We hoped that we were not trying to give the public too much of a good thing. After all, a third series was a rather daring experiment for a public notoriously changeable in its tastes. . . .

CHAPTER XIV

ITMA COMES INTO ITS OWN

IF, in the following chapters, I trace ITMA to its end in 1949, it is to show that it was a contemporary document ; it followed the trend of events during the war years and after. It will, I hope, revive many memories of him, and will show how Tommy worked for the enlivenment of his ever-growing multitude of listeners, and how he helped to sustain national morale throughout the darkest days. It was during these years that he grew so greatly in stature, that he became a great public figure, a household name. From now on the *tempo* of his life rapidly progresses from *presto* to *prestissimo* with the inevitable consequences which I have already described.

After less than two months' break, the new series of ITMA started on September 25th, 1941. It was a more cheerful period for the British people. Since the German attack on Russia three months earlier the armies of the Nazis were at last rumbling to an apparent standstill, and although the rout of the Italians in North and East Africa had been followed by the arrival of Rommel's Afrika Corps, the news was no longer almost undilutedly bad. ITMA could well afford to foster the growing feeling of optimism in the nation.

We had some discussion about the theme of the next series, and Tommy was greatly in favour of remaining at Foaming-at-the Mouth. And so, the series followed much the same routine as the previous short group of programmes. The first programme of the new series opened with some of the best-loved of the characters— Claude and Cecil and Sam Scram and Lefty. They prepared the official welcome for the return of the Mayor. When he alighted from the train Tommy immediately introduced his latest acquisition—Signor So So, his foreign secretary. The part was, of course, played brilliantly by Dino Galvani. Another famous character was the cheery commercial played by Clarence Wright. In this programme he made his début with : " Good morning—nice day !—could I interest you in a little insurance ? No ? I'll call again. Good morning, Nice day ! "

Tommy explained that the caller was Percy Premium, the Policy Pusher. In his innumerable visits which were to follow, he always had another name. He was back within five minutes on this occasion as Stan the Stationery Man, selling carbon papers, typewriter ribbons and rubber stamps. Reaction to the first programme, in which Tommy had some trouble with his Corporation who did their best to unseat him, indicated that Signor So-So was already proving popular. The idea had been to make him a rather fatuous Italian version of Funf, but there was little sinister about his falsetto querying voice or his obvious admiration of Signor Handlebar. So from the second programme his remarks became more and more benign and more decidedly wrong. From the start of Programme Two of the new series, Tommy gave So-So a big job to run his new Twelve Week Plan. The first blue prints showed fountains in the streets, piazzas everywhere, and yet it was—" nothing at all, nothing at all," as So-So put it.

There was a little interlude in the programme

broadcast on October 10th. In the script the sequence appears like this :

(Door opens—clatter of bucket.)

DOROTHY SUMMERS : Can I do for you now, sir ?

TOM :   I've been done for already. Who may you be ?

DOROTHY : The Town Clerk said you needed a washer.

TOM :   Well, I can't tie you on the tap ; I'm on tap myself.

DOROTHY : He sent me here to scrub you out.

TOM :   Now, wasn't that nice of him ! You can tell the Town Clerk I don't need scrubbing out or pumping out.

DOROTHY : Can't I even wash round your skirting ?

TOM :   You come an inch closer and I'll kick your bucket. Who are you, anyhow ?

DOROTHY : I'm Mrs. Mopp, the Corporation cleanser.

We didn't get her famous catch phrase exactly right that time—later it became " Can I do you now, sir ? " —and her gift to the Mayor was missing. Her farewell was not composed of initials (T.T.F.N.), but was just a chummy " Toodle-oo, Mr. Mayor." If she had known the long series of conversations she was starting with this programme she might not have been so brief in her interview with her new master, but during the following week we learned from our post bag that Mrs. Mopp must stay. In the following broadcast she was promoted to the first position in the programme, with a sequence right after Tommy's " Hello, Folks ! " It was clear that she had liked the Mayor on her previous week's visit, for this time she brought him a little gift. Tommy's imagination in the weekly guessing game was not so good then as it became by practice, for all he said was : " A pot of jam ? "

And Mrs. Mopp replied : " Yes, sir—it's carrot jelly.

Those with good memories will recall how the Ministry of Food was, that autumn and winter, advertising the virtues of carrots in every conceivable form.   They could be used instead of marmalade ; they could be eaten raw instead of sweets ; they would enable you to see better in the dark.   Mrs. Mopp's gift, though strained through her jumper, was at least a patriotic one.   And here we gained our first plaudit from the Government, for our assistance in the great carrot campaign—it was to be the first of many.   The routine was simple.

(Door opens.)

VOICE :   Do you know what you can do with a carrot ?
TOMMY :   Yes.

(Door closes.)

That was all.

By the time the fifth programme of the series was broadcast, Tommy was getting probably the biggest audience ever known by the variety artistes on the B.B.C.   The transmission details were by now set out as :

HOME AND FORCES : 24th October, 8.30-9 p.m.
RECORD REPEAT (FORCES) : 26th October, 8.30-9 a.m.
REPRODUCTION FOR EMPIRE—PACIFIC : 4th November, 8-8.30 a.m.   NORTH AMERICA : 7th November, 10.30-11 p.m.

There was, of course, no Listener Research organisation on the scale of to-day, and therefore no estimated figures based on a cross section enquiry of listeners was forthcoming. But it was suggested at the time that with these four separate broadcasts Tommy had an audience exceeding 16,000,000.

Sam Costa, by now in the R.A.F., dropped into this programme with a bit of true-to-life dialogue. He was as cheeky as ever, though Tommy hardly recognised his one-time office boy because he'd had a wash, grown a moustache, and his feet were bigger—a reference to the R.A.F.'s ground staff. Sam's visit gave Tommy an idea, though. He decided to declare Martial Law in Foaming-at-the-Mouth. To whip up military enthusiasm in the town Tom showed a film entitled " Half Shot at Dawn," a reconstruction of the Great Canteen Campaign of 1899. This, of course, took place somewhere in the far-flung Empire, and there was a significant little piece of dialogue when an orderly came galloping in on an elephant.

" Chit for Colonel Chinstrap. Chit for Colonel Chinstrap," shouted Sam. Tommy, as Captain, took the message and opened it himself. It was, he explained, as much as his commission was worth to awaken the Colonel The listeners did not, therefore, hear the Colonel speak on that programme. There was nothing in the script for him. As a matter of fact, even if there had been no one would have heard it. This was the only ITMA programme which was faded out by the B.B.C. because of enemy action. In October, 1941, the Luftwaffe had turned from attacking London to start sporadic attacks on provincial towns, large or small.

In the hall at Bangor that night everyone could hear distant gunfire, and we had been warned that there was an alert. In the way that these things happened just at the time when the distant noise started the dialogue went on like this :

Tommy and Company arrive at Scapa Flow and are seen on the deck of H.M.S. *Anson*, January 1944

A furniture van was the only transport available when Tommy broadcast *Itma* from the Garrison Theatre, Woolwich, in 1944

"Where are you going to, my pretty maid?" Tommy is all dressed up in buttons and bows

With Horace Percival (the Diver) and Dorothy Summers. Broadcast to
America in *Atlantic Spotlight*, February 1944

V—I.T.M.A.

Tommy joins the famous and infamous—as he is sculpted for Madame Tussaud's by E. Whitney Smith

An *Itma* rehearsal, 1947

"Let's get this straight," says Tommy to Jack Train (Colonel Chinstrap)

"It's being so cheerful as keeps me going!" moans Joan Harben (Mona Lott)

For five years Tommy dodged Miss Hotchkiss, who pursued him from
pillar to post

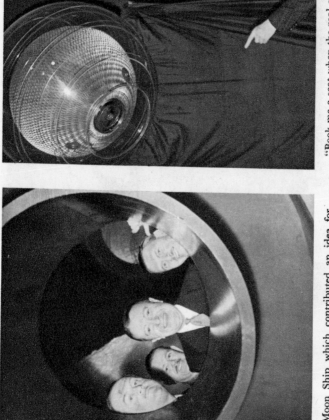

The Moon Ship which contributed an idea for *Itma*, but never got nearer the Moon than Tomtopia. (With Tommy, Francis and myself is the designer, Warnett Kennedy)

"Book me a seat when the real one is ready," said Tommy

Teenie Goss, the producer's secretary, saw us through many crises from 1940 to 1949

TOM :   Now we shall want some entanglements—
             so you'd better get hold of the two girls.
             Now what else do we want, Sam ?

SAM :   Guns, Boss, guns !

DOROTHY :   No guns.

TOM :   All right—we'll have a pound of butter.
                    (*Door opens.*)

TOM :   Well, I'll go to Bedlam. My two beauty
             queens in uniform already !

PAULA :   They aren't half smart they ain't 'arf.

KAY :   I think mine is positively revolting——

TOM :   I must say I like accordion pleated trousers.
             A bit brief in the bivouac—but a nice piece
             of pinking round the pandemonium. Do
             you know what to do in case of attack ?

KAY :   It's not exactly what you do—it's the way
             you perform it.

PAULA :   'S'right—it ain't what you do—it's the way
             that you do it.
                    (*Cue for song.*)

The two girls, Paula Green and Kay Cavendish, started to sing the song. There were two loud explosions, and then utter silence. Glass tinkled from the roof and from some windows in the building. Dust rose in a cloud. The two girls did not falter, but went on singing, and the programme continued for a few minutes. We in the studio did not know that instantly the crash came over the microphone the programme had been faded by some control engineer far away at the transmitter and gramophone records put on until they overcame the " technical hitch." The explosions were caused by parachute mines, probably intended for the shipping lanes in Liverpool, but dropped by the enemy planes on Bangor, causing considerable damage and killing a driver of one of the B.B.C. cars.

But by the following week it was business as usual at Foaming-in-the-Mouth, with Tommy engaged in organising a night club, the Mayor's Nest, in the lowest part of the High Street. Tommy, by adroit eavesdropping on a 'phone where the lines were crossed, was able to hear Funf and So-So talking. Like their masters at the time, who were squabbling over the mess-up in Africa, and all was not well with the Axis arrangements.

So-So : But I am doing my best.
Funf :   Of everything you make the mess-up. You are finito-finito.
So-So : Benito—Benito.
Funf :   I give you just one more chance.

It was a slice of ITMA that considerably annoyed the monitors of the German and Italian broadcasting services, for their propaganda sections were busily putting out optimistic stories of the happy discussions between the two dictators at the time.

In the programme on November 14th, Maurice Denham, now a Major, came along during army leave to lend a hand. He played the part of Mrs. Tickle again, explaining to Tommy that she had gone on the land, since marrying a farmer. It was characteristic of Tommy, who kept in touch with everyone who went into the services from the cast, the band or the technical and production staff, that he should insist on Maurice having a chance of doing a little broadcasting when military duties permitted, just as he had for Sam Costa. It also provided a delightful scene between the two charwomen. Maurice, as Lola Tickle, was left alone in the office and decided to clean it up. The door opened as she wielded her duster.

MRS. MOPP : And what may you be a doin' of may I ask ?

MRS. TICKLE : I'm tidying up this filthy office for Mr. Itma.

MRS. MOPP : Oh, you are, are you ? Let me tell you, I do for His Worship, and no one else.

MRS. TICKLE : I always do my best for all my gentlemen.

MRS. MOPP : Then you won't do it in here. I'm Mrs. Mopp, the Corporation Cleaner.

MRS. TICKLE : And I'm Lola Tickle, Mr. Itma's fancy.

MRS. MOPP : Tickle by name and tickle by nature, no doubt.

MRS. TICKLE : Don't you cast excursions at me, Mrs. Mopp.

MRS. MOPP : And don't you dust my gentleman's doings, Mrs. Tickle.

MRS. TICKLE : He's mine—I did for him first.

MRS. MOPP : He's used to ladies' attention, and you're no lady.

MRS. TICKLE : You're a woman—that's what you are Mrs. Mopp. A woman.

As they started to pull each other's hair down, Tommy came in and said : " Here, what's all this ? Scratch as cat's can ? Now come on, kiss and be friends."

" I'm resigning, your washup," said Mrs. Mopp, " and I'll sue you for ali-money."

" I don't worry about Japanese Admirals," Tommy replied. That was in the programme of November 14th, 1941. Just over three weeks later came the attack on Pearl Harbour. It was one of the rare occasions when a gag by Tommy was hardly appropriate, though he couldn't have known it at the time, of course, for the Japanese had delegates holding out olive branches in

Washington while their fleet was steaming to its war stations.

Tommy had a very busy time over the Christmas season. He had a broadcast on Boxing Day, and another on January 2nd. In the first months of 1942 Foaming-in-the-Mouth had its Warship Week, its Bomber Week, even its Tomship Week. The black market was attacked. Plans for de-housing after the war were finalised. The inefficient characters with which he had surrounded himself kept Tommy continually at work giving them the opportunities for their by now famous lines. It was phenomenal the way they had caught on among all sections of the community. At first we started to make a collection of the instances which were sent to us by letters. They became too numerous, but there are a few which Tommy kept with pride that he had in some measure contributed to the lightening of the burden of the war.

Many of them concerned incidents where humour emerged from the brutality of total war. There was, for example, the letter from the head of a demolition squad. His men had been called to a house which had received a direct hit. He clambered over the pile of rubble which had once been a little home in Bath.

" Anyone there ? " he called as he flashed his torch here and there.

" Yes," piped a small boy lying buried under the debris. " Can you do me now, sir ? " Doctors and nurses wrote of the victims of bombs who, knowing that death was coming, murmured T.T.F.N. as the last coherent thing they said. It was the commonplace joke of an indomitable people. Cecil and Claude's ultra-polite conversation and consideration for one another's convenience became a catch phrase with servicemen.

Pilots of bombers queueing up over a target would shout it over the inter-com. to one another as they manœuvred for the bombing run. Merchant Navy men and air crews would whisper it with voices almost gone through thirst as the rescue launches came alongside their rafts and lifeboats.

People wrote just to say how the ITMA programmes lightened the gloom of war, and comparatively few of these people had any sort of request to make. They did, as I have mentioned elsewhere, receive a reply from Tommy, who spent hour after hour reading every one of them. Often, if security regulations permitted, Tommy would include just a few words of patter which was really just a message to some correspondent, and would be appreciated fully only by that listener. After all his years on the stage, during which time he had received his share of applause, or fan-worship as we would call it to-day, he still remained amazed and even a little bewildered at the colossal success of ITMA. The reason is not that one does not realise that a particular radio programme has " clicked " ; it would be false modesty to say otherwise. But it is virtually impossible to appreciate the size of a radio audience. When figures get into tens of millions the imagination baulks at assessing this in terms of human beings. Although the letters that came represented the merest fraction of the listening public, they did bring home the variety of people who listened to ITMA, and the enormous area of the world which it reached.

It was at one of our daily letter-reading sessions in Francis Worsley's office at Bangor that Tommy suddenly exclaimed : " Well, I'll go to the foot of our stairs."

He took out his handkerchief and wiped his forehead— a characteristic gesture of his when excited or moved—

then he got his glasses out of their case, put them on and read the letter again. Neither Francis nor I showed unusual interest, for Tommy was a confirmed addict to the habit of reading bits of letters and newspaper articles aloud, sometimes making them up as he went along. I think we both imagined that he had heard from an old friend with whom he had lost touch for some years. ITMA brought him many such reunions.

This time he didn't read the letter aloud. He passed it across to us. This was what we saw :

WINDSOR CASTLE

2nd March, 1942.

PRIVATE AND CONFIDENTIAL.

Tommy Handley, Esq.,
c/o B.B.C.,
Bangor, Caerns,
N. Wales.

DEAR SIR,

The King and Queen have expressed the desire to see a performance of your Company.

As you are in Wales and not knowing what your professional engagements may be, I do not know whether it would be possible to arrange a performance at Windsor next month. An appropriate date would be about the 21st April, which is Princess Elizabeth's birthday.

If this could be arranged without serious inconvenience to yourself and your company, I would suggest that if you have an Agent in London he might come down to Windsor Castle and see the hall which is used for such entertainments. I wish to stress that Their Majesties particularly desire that there should be no interference with any of your professional engagements.

Will you kindly treat this letter as strictly confidential.

Yours truly,
(*Signed*) **P. W. LEGH.**
Master of the Household.

(Printed by permission.)

Tommy watched our faces as we read and re-read the letter. Then he said : " I suppose it can't be a joke ? " He knew his own activities with spurious names on 'phone calls and postcards. There wasn't any joke about his, however. The note-heading was proof of that.

We were at the time busy on the final touches of the script for broadcasting on March 6th, which was concerned with spring cleaning at the Mayor's parlour. If that programme wasn't quite up to standard we may be forgiven, for the rest of the morning the script was forgotten—and so, indeed, was lunch.

It was Francis Worsley's secretary, Teenie Goss, one of the dozens of people whose names never appeared in the list of credits for ITMA, but without whose help it would never have gone on the air without a hitch as it managed to do year after year, who restored us to normal.

" I don't think any of you have had any lunch," she said. " And, Tommy, if you are not careful you'll miss the post with your mother's letter."

This was the day when Tommy sent his weekly diary to his mother. He picked up the letter from the desk, and said : " What a pity I can't tell her yet. She'd be

tickled to death to have this news. Maybe she'll remember how I used to say one day I would be the
King's Jester when I was reading fairy story books by
the fire at home."

Francis went off to London for a personal interview
with the King's Equerry, Sir Piers Legh, and on his
return we learned that something quite elaborate was
envisaged. The programme was to last two hours and
was to be given in the Waterloo Chamber at Windsor
Castle, complete with microphones, red lights, and all
the rest of the studio atmosphere. ITMA, we considered, could be amplified to last forty minutes, compared with the half-hour it had on the ordinary broadcast, and we invited other artistes to precede our own
part of the programme. As a number of the Guards
stationed at the Castle were to be in the audience, one
certain choice was Robb Wilton in his Home Guard
sketch ; then there was Jack Warner from Garrison
Theatre ; Vera Lynn, the sweetheart of the forces ;
Kenway and Young, and Max Geldray—a wonderful
harmonica player over here in the Dutch Army.

Francis and I got the script for the ordinary ITMA
broadcast on March 13th all complete, and left it with
Tommy while we made a quick journey to Windsor
Castle—Francis to see the arrangements in the Castle,
and I to pick up some local atmosphere.

The theme of the show was that Tommy was himself
having a birthday party. We submitted the script for
official approval ; it came back with a statement that
everything was in order, and we were ready for our
journey. The whole party went by train to London,
and then by coaches to Windsor.

For the first time in his life, I should say, Tommy
was really nervous. He was quieter on that trip than

I had ever known him, but by the time we had " de-bussed " outside the large gates in to the Castle grounds which we had been told to use, the old Tommy was back in form.

Francis pulled the massive bell handle, and after the clanging had died away an imposing figure opened a side door and looked at the strange collection of rather pallid people grouped there.

" We are the party from the B.B.C.," explained Francis.

The footman seemed a little doubtful, when from the centre of the crowd came the familiar Lancashire voice : " Got any digs ? "

The poker-faced royal servant grinned suddenly. " Oh, it's you, Mr. Handley," he said. " Come this way."

We had arrived fairly early in the morning. We immediately started a rehearsal to see that everything would run smoothly. The band tuned up, and Charlie Shadwell raised his baton to play the familiar opening bars of the signature tune, when an official hurried in.

" Stop, please," he said. " You really cannot play here." The reason, it appeared, after our completely blank faces had shown him that this was, to say the least of it, an unusual order, was that the inspection of the Guards which Princess Elizabeth was going to take as Colonel-in-Chief was just outside the Waterloo Chamber. Obviously the sound of " It's That Man Again " would spoil things. But the rehearsal had to go on, and it did. The orchestra went through all the motions of playing their numbers without making a sound— the strangest full-dress rehearsal on record. But it did enable us to time the programme.

At lunch-time we were conducted into the room of the Gentlemen of the Household, where a buffet was laid out on long tables with footmen waiting to serve the meal. The Gentlemen were waiting to receive us— a little stiff and dubious about the people from this crazy world of radio make-believe. The two groups tended to huddle together. Once again Tommy came to the rescue.

" Nice little place you've got here," he said. " What's the grub like ? " looking round one of the loveliest rooms he or I had probably ever seen in our lives. The ice was broken. Within a few minutes everyone was chatting like old friends.

The conversation during that lunch provided us with a lot more local colour, and in the afternoon Tommy simply poured out ideas for me to develop. How he managed to learn all the amusing anecdotes of practi- cally everyone on the staff of the Castle in the time he had I do not know. But the fact remains that he had collected a mass of gossipy information on nick- names, whims and characteristics of people from the officers of the guard down to under-footmen. That was yet another of his notable qualities—he could walk with Kings and talk with Commoners—and feel at home with any of them.

Tommy worked harder on that show than any in his life. His own act needed plenty of work. But more than that he welded the cast into the perfect team it was in its ordinary broadcasts. It would be foolish to say that the nerves that we all felt when we first arrived had evaporated by mid-afternoon. But by sheer person- ality and suggestion, Tommy broke down the tautness of some of the artistes. He had them laughing and fooling. At last, when there was a particular burst of horseplay he turned to me and winked. I knew what he meant. The ITMA team he knew and loved, the team that put on the weekly show, was back in form. We were ready for the curtain to go up.

The hall seated a considerable number of people. The troops, representative of all the Guards' Regiments stationed at the Castle (which was not merely a barracks for the Royal Household but a strategic station for training and defence against invasion) came in first, and then the officers who had seats at the front. They noticed that some of the men had to stand. They got up, in the best tradition of the most disciplined unit in the British Army, told the men to take the seats and stood themselves. Then the various members of the Household entered, and finally, as the whole audience stood up, the King, the Queen, and the two Princesses arrived.

John Watt had come down to supervise the whole show, and John Snagge to compere it. As soon as the Royal Family were seated the order was given to dim the lights in the auditorium. Someone must have been completely overcome by the momentous occasion, for he snapped the master switch and the whole place went into complete blackness. It looked like a bad start. Actually, as Tommy whispered to me where we stood watching in the wings, it wasn't. He was right. As soon as things were remedied and the stage again became bathed in light, everyone laughed. The tense, formal atmosphere was gone. That electrician had " warmed the house " for the first turn, which was given by Kenway and Young. All the separate acts went very well, and then came the moment we had been awaiting. John Snagge explained that the show about to begin would be an exact replica of the ITMA broadcast. The red light flashed, the curtain went up, the Jeep (Junior programme engineer in charge of effects) stood ready with the ITMA door and his equipment of coconut shells, tin cans and rattles, and Tommy walked on the stage.

Now it so happened that in the general excitement of preparing the show none of us had worried very much about the costume for Tommy as Mayor of Foaming-in-the-Mouth. It had not, I fear, occurred to us that as this was a visual broadcast a neat lounge suit or evening dress would hardly be appropriate for a blundering, incompetent Mayor of a third-rate resort. That would have been carrying realism of a broadcast too far.

But Tommy had thought of this. From somewhere he had obtained a moth-eaten frock coat and a mayoral chain of office composed of every bit of plumbing and ironware he could lay his hands on in the ironmongery shops and garages of Bangor. On his head was a top hat several sizes too small for him.

From the word " Go ! " there was laughter all along the line. In fact, if it had been broadcast, there would have been complaints about the noise of the studio audience drowning the dialogue. But as it was, every word that couldn't be heard after a topical joke was just another feather in our cap. The biggest laugh of the show came in the Mrs. Mopp interlude.

Mrs. Mopp wandered in and said, " I—I brought this for you, sir."

" What is it ? " Tommy asked. " Snapper Robinson's chest ? "

The ensuing dialogue insinuated that it might be the Crown Jewels, but no one heard them. The allusion to the medals on the staunchest, broadest, proudest chest in the Guards stationed at Windsor, that of the R.S.M., brought the house down.

The forty minutes went very quickly—a sure sign of success, and after the final applause and the final curtain we breathed a sigh of relief at a job quite well done and now finished. But it wasn't quite the end of this notable occasion. The door of the room we had been allocated for our preparations opened and an equerry came in.

"Will Mr. Handley, and the cast, the variety acts, the conductor, and producer, together with Mr. Watt, Mr. Snagge, Mr. Kavanagh, come to the ante-room, please."

We put out our cigarettes, straightened our ties, and followed the manservant who was there to direct us. It was rather awe-inspiring, for we were lined up in a long narrow room with two doors at either end. We automatically thought of the Guards' inspection we had glimpsed in the grounds.

Then one of the doors opened and in trotted two dogs —a Corgi and a Scottie.

They did the inspection, sniffing from one to another of us right down the line. Then they got bored and lay down to sleep. There was a rustle of movement, and the Queen came in, followed by the King, with the Princesses behind. They had a chat with everyone present, and both the King and Queen told Tommy how disappointed they were to learn that ITMA was coming off the air that Spring. The Queen asked him if it would be resumed, and when he said that it would she smilingly commented, " Ah, you go—you come back."

It was a delightful gesture to complete our feeling of a perfect day, and, as Tommy mentioned when we were back in Bangor, the memory of that place will be a souvenir of ITMA for ever. It's a pity that we couldn't have had some photos just as a tangible something to keep " and show Jean and Mother."

Photographs were, of course, taboo, at a time when

the whereabouts of the Royal Family was Top Secret, but we did get the tangible souvenir Tommy wanted— each of us received a set of records, in a leather-bound album, lettered in gold : " Windsor Castle, 21st April, 1942," and autographed by the Family. The microphone we had used to amplify our voices in the hall and give the radio atmosphere to the show had been wired to recorders by arrangement with the B.B.C. engineers, and this magnificent present was the Royal Family's way of thanking us.

I think that the times when Tommy was able to play those records over at home for Jean and later for his Mother in Liverpool, were always counted by him as one of the happiest in his life.

The signatures of the Royal Family as they appear in the album of records.

CHAPTER XV

FROM WINDSOR CASTLE TO SCAPA FLOW

A S we were sworn to secrecy before the Royal ITMA
and were asked to refrain from publicity afterwards, there was little mention in the Press of this great
occasion. It had not been broadcast, indeed, as it was
on rather broader lines than the usual show, and as it
was a privileged show this was the one ITMA the listener
did not hear. To Tommy, in retrospect, it seemed a
kind of dream. He often referred to it, and when he
met the Royal Family and broadcast to them again,
he told them that for once in his life he was not nervous.
They were so friendly, so appreciative and so obviously
au fait with ITMA that his nerves disappeared and he
felt perfectly at home.

However, he couldn't rest on his laurels. The visit
to Windsor had been the greatest event of his life, and
he hurried home to tell Jean all about it while the rest
of us made a night of it in London. The next morning
there was another edition to write, another series to line
up. There was no question of the signal honour given
to Tommy, the historical importance of the first Royal
Radio Command, giving him a swollen head ; it made
him realise his responsibilities more than ever. ITMA
mustn't just be good—it must be better, and it was in
this spirit that he faced the next series.

When the time came for it to begin in September,
1942, listeners met all their old friends in the same
old place—Foaming-in-the-Mouth. However, it soon

appeared that the long-suffering citizenry of that resort
had at last done something about the corrupt administration of the town, and Tom received his marching
orders. He did, as a matter of fact, continue his municipal
duties in a rather vague and undefined capacity, but
the accent of the show after the first two broadcasts was
on war production. Tommy, like tens of millions of
his listeners, was seen to be busy on war work in one
of the massive new factories which were by then getting
into full running order, piling up material for the imminent attack in the Western Desert and the still far-off
Second Front.

Although this factory was easily the most inefficient in
the world—it never managed to produce anything,
although it received orders for tanks, battleships, big
guns and bombs—the general atmosphere and jargon
used in the show was authentic. During the summer
before the show began Francis and I paid a visit to the
Wellington bomber works at Chester, and it was from
this visit that we picked up the slang phrases and routine
used in the show. I found, too, that my long experience
in making industrial films came in handy.

The versatile employees of the Mayor's Parlour quickly
adapted themselves to factory work, and even Funf
managed to come along as well. He brought a friend
with him, a jovial spy named Johann Bull (Fred Yule),
full of heavy Teutonic humour and a misplaced sense
of horse-play with bombs and booby traps. Signor So-
So, now one of the big attractions of the show, took up
medicine and was responsible for the general health of
the factory employees. He and Tommy started a routine
which seemed to delight everyone. Here is an excerpt
from the show on October 2nd, when the spelling gag
was first introduced :

So-So : Ah, Mr. Hangnail, you sent for me ? Again you have an attack of the anni domini—yes ?

Tom : No ; only a touch of the titti-folols—a kind of concert party on the chest. I want a thorough overhaul, Dr. So-So.

So-So : First, I test your blood. You're anæmic.

Tom : No, you're thinking of Jack Train. He's a mimic.

So-So : I think you glup your food.

Tom : Glup my food ? You mean gulp my food ?

So-So : Yes—glup your food.

Tom : Listen—G-U-L-P—Glup.

So-So : You mean—gulp—now I feel your plus.

Another amusing character who made his *debut* in this programme was Norman the Doorman, ex-usher of the Handleydrome (again played by Fred Yule). " Viccy verky " was his catch phrase. He had some close competition for popularity from Bookham, the Variety Agent, who finished most of his sentences with the remark, " Wo-ho "—a further feather in the cap of the versatile Jack Train.

A very successful programme was broadcast in October, when Tommy collected his board of directors. It was a means of introducing to listeners Mr. Luke Smart, the tailor, who sniffed his way through his dialogue, and the immortal Colonel Chinstrap, at last with a speaking part. Most people will probably have forgotten that it was Tommy who twisted the Colonel's remarks to the name of a drink in most of the early sequences of this series of programmes, as happened with the first words of conversation the two had together. Jack Train came through the door and said : " Apologies and all that, Handley. Just had your wire—delighted to join your board. I think you should have another . . ."

F

To which, of course, Tommy replied : " Have another ? Thanks, I will."

Then there was the Man from the Ministry—what branch of Whitehall he came from was as mysterious as the purpose of Tommy's factory. He was played by Clarence Wright, and had a curious trick of repeating the last words of the sentence, like this :

" Oh, Mr. Handley, I believe—I said Mr. Handley, I believe. I've come to look at your factory—I said look at your factory." This character was, by the way, a discovery of Francis Worsley's, and was based on his conversation with a soldier he met late one night who wanted to know the way to his billet. He talked in precisely the way the Man from the Ministry did, and seemed quite unaware of his habit. Francis walked along with him and soon found that he was talking in the same manner. When he told Tommy and me about it on the following morning it seemed like a gift for the show—one of the few characters (The Diver, as already related, was another) in which we didn't have to invent but found ready-made.

The abbreviated farewells of Mrs. Mopp became so well-known that most people would think that they were as old as the character. Actually the idea was developed quite late in the day, though on looking over the scripts I have noticed that as early as October 30th Tommy asked her (during one of his discussions on her proposed enlistment in work of greater national importance than that available in Tommy's establishment) : " What are you joining, Mrs. Mopp ? The T.T.F.N.'s ? " Frankly, I cannot recall why this was used at this stage, and Mrs. Mopp certainly did not ask what it stood for. She was, of course, saying " Ta-ta for now " at the end of each interview, and it was then and for many weeks to come) Tommy's practice to reply with a rhyming line such as " Aren't you a wow ? "

Another landmark was created on November 6th, when the programme was broadcast for the first time to the Forces in the Middle East and West Africa. In the autumn of 1942 enormous masses of men were gathering in the Western Desert, and there was no secret in the fact that one of the big battles of the war was coming along within a few weeks. Rommel had pushed to the borders of Egypt, Churchill had been on one of his famous war-time trips to the Middle East, and everything was ready to go up on a very big show. Tommy was very delighted that ITMA was to be heard by the tens of thousands of men waiting and preparing for El Alamein. By his own request there was a special line of dialogue in the middle of the show to let the men of the M.E.F. know what the folks at home thought about them. Mr. Bookham came in and said :

" Good news for you, Mr. H. Great good news."

" What ? " exclaimed Tommy. " Have you heard from the Middle East already ? "

Later, in a 'phone chat with Funf, Tommy got another big laugh with the line : " When you see Hitler ask him if I can get one of Rommel's remnants without any coupons."

Topicality became a strong feature of the programme. People started to look for lines which were as fresh as that night's news. It meant a lot of last-minute alterations, but the trouble was worth it, and Tommy had a quick ear for a topical reference. On November 20th Sam Scram burst in with the query : " Boss, boss, have you heard the wonderful news from Libya ? "

" Of course I have," Tommy replied. " What's the Mersa Matruth ? Have you heard the news from

Algiers? It's turned out Eisenhow, hasn't it?" This referred, of course, to the American successes in the North African landings, and was a play on a slogan of George Doonan's "What's the matter with you?" And "turned out Eisenhow" was a twist on "It's turned out nice again."

As the British armies swept across the Western Desert the hearty Johann Bull had a tough job to keep up his laboured humour in his disarming chats with Tommy.

"Heard from Rommel lately?" asked Tommy.

"Rommel?" said Johann. "He is only a joke."

"I wish you'd tell me where he's stopping," Tommy added. "My pal Montgomery wants a word with him."

There was other big news beside the war developments at that time in the winter of 1942. The Beveridge Plan of social security was issued. Tommy duly appeared as His Fatuity the Minister of Social Hilarity, explaining : "I've been up the last three days and nights reading the first chapter of a book called 'Gone With the Want,' by that stout fellow Beveridge."

But there was still opportunity for war references. Announcers were faced in every news bulletin with most improbable names of towns and railway junctions in Western Russia, and one of the places which for some reason registered in the public's mind was Velikiluki captured by the Red Army on January 1st. Tommy was unkind enough to enquire of Funf whether his address was now The Retreat, Velikiluki. "Get to the other side of the Don, will you?" Tommy added. And Funf truthfully admitted that he would have to retire immediately. Ali Oop, the Levantine pedlar, also tried to sell him a hot-water bottle "Very Veleaky, very Veluki."

ITMA was broadcast on Christmas Day and got an additional five minutes to include the extra music which was included in the factory party. It also finished with a special announcement which stated : " Lots of people have written wanting to know what characters are played by whom, so as a sort of belated Christmas present here are the most regular ones . . ."

This announcement had really become necessary to help the overworked and depleted clerical staff of the B.B.C. Letters were arriving by the sackful asking for decisions on various arguments, and in some cases it was stated vehemently that a reply was urgently needed because bets had been placed. The majority of listeners could not understand how the ten supporting players were able to match up with twenty or more characters, and this applies particularly to the various roles played by Jack Train and Horace Percival. It may be of interest to devotees of the early ITMA programmes to reproduce the script which was used as the vocal " Who's who on Christmas Day, 1942." Here it is :

ANNOUNCER :   Jack Train plays Claude, Lefty, Funf, and the convivial Colonel. Like the rest of the cast he plays many another one.

TRAIN :   Another one ? I don't mind if I do.

ANNOUNCER :   Dino Galvani plays Signor So-So.

GALVANI :   Yes, I am amphibious. I love all the ladies.

ANNOUNCER :   Fred Yule plays Norman the Doorman, and Johann Bull.

YULE :   Just for a little choke.

ANNOUNCER :   Horace Percival plays Cecil, Ali Oop, and——

PERCIVAL :   Don't forget the diver, sir, don't forget the diver.

ANNOUNCER :   Clarence Wright plays Inspector Squirt
               and——
WRIGHT :   Good morning. Nice day.
ANNOUNCER :   Dorothy Summers is Mrs. Mopp, the
               faithful charwoman.
DOROTHY :   I've brought this for him, sir.
ANNOUNCER :   Sydney Keith plays Sam Scram.
KEITH :   Well, for evermore.
ANNOUNCER :   Vera Lennox plays the flirtatious factory
               girl.
VERA :   Ooh, Mr. Handley, I think you're wizard.
ANNOUNCER :   And of course Tommy Handley is always
               mother's pride and joy, Mrs. Handley's
               boy.

This special announcement stemmed the avalanche of
letters for a little while, but people's memories are short,
and we were soon getting as many arguments to settle
as ever.

The series finished on January 29th, when Tommy
announced he had received orders to disperse the factory.
It was followed by an omnibus edition a week later of
the music used in the series, compered by Tommy.
It made a pleasant little half-hour programme, and
enabled Tommy to say some nice things about the
arrangers—Henry Reed, Gordon Jacobs, Arthur Sand-
ford, and Clive Richardson. ITMA had broken new
ground with the adroit inclusion of musical items which
became part of the show and followed on easily from
the dialogue between Tommy and Charlie Shadwell,
the most insulted conductor in the world.

With the closing bars of this musical extra Tommy
came to the microphone and said : " T.T.T.A."—" Ta-
ta till April."

CHAPTER XVI

THE new series got off to a flying start on April 15th, 1943. Tommy had spent the interval in visiting camps, aerodromes, hospitals and factories, sometimes alone, sometimes with Jack Train, Clarry Wright or other " Itma-ites." No unit was too small, no camp too remote for him to go to and, in addition, he did many broadcasts—by himself or with Ronald Frankau. There was a new lilt about war-time life in Britain, and we did our best to reflect it in the show. In the few weeks that we had been off the air good news had been rolling in all the time. In Tunisia the weight of two converging forces were crushing the hemmed-in enemy, Berlin was getting heavy night raids—and 8,000 tons of bombs went down on the Reich in the previous month of March. And just before the broadcast came the flash that the 8th Army and the U.S. 2nd Corps had made contact in North Africa.

All this good news made even the Budget, with its 100 per cent. purchase tax on luxury goods, and increased duties on tobacco and the Colonel's food, bearable. Tommy discovered this to be true in his first chat with his friend, who complained gently :

" Why must the Chancellor always tax necessities ? Another penny a pint, sir—that's an extra five shillings a day. It's a terrible burden."

" Burton ? " asked Tommy. " I'll have a small quart."

" Small port ? " said the Colonel eagerly.

" Pour it in as well," agreed Tom.

Tommy was, of course, still running his factory, but on account of his misgivings as to its efficiency, he rang up Dr. Joad (played, on this occasion only, by Jack Train). The Brains Trust expert advised Tommy on the future of his factory. He said : " In answer to your query regarding your works or factory I would advise you to hide your discrepancies by placing your factory or works underground, thus economising space and concealing your—if I may say so—rather underhand methods."

It was rather brutal advice, but Tommy took it. He made the first thrust with the spade and instantly struck a well. He'd struck an idea, too, a suggestion to turn the factory into a health spa, and this was the theme of the following week's show. This broadcast introduced Miss Pansy Cowe-Parsley, fresh air fiend and nature lover. Tommy parried her advice on health foods quite well, but the woman enraged the Colonel to a frenzy. " Who is this hag, Handley ? "

She was followed by Tommy's old friend who never finished a sentence, another role for Horace Percival. This character, Mr. Whats'isname was one of the most amusing yet annoying in the ITMA repertoire. Tommy delighted us one day with an account of just such a person whom he had met at a London station on a visit to town. He gave a perfect cameo (doubtless with suitable fictional elaborations) of the way the conversation went, and I saw that here was a tailor-made character to add to the show. He made his *debut* on April 22nd, when Lefty let him through the door of the Spa Director's office :

HORACE : Hello, Handley . . . you remember me, don't you?

TOM : Yes—I—did you have a beard then?

HORACE : No. I used to wear one of those you knows.

TOM : Oh, a sort of——

HORACE : Yes—when we were in—er——

TOM : That place with a——

HORACE : That's it—the landlady had a——

TOM : Of course. What happened to her—er——

HORACE : Oh, you mean her—er—I think she ran away with the er——

TOM : That's the man who used to stay here. Tall fellow with a black-handled penknife.

HORACE : Went on tour with a show called—you remember.

TOM : Good heavens, yes. We opened at——

HORACE : Yes, but only for the first week. After that we went to——

TOM : Played a fortnight there—or was it three weeks?

HORACE : Oh no. That was in—you know the place——

TOM : Where the Main Street ran sideways——

HORACE : Yes, you left us after that. Didn't you join the——

TOM : No—that was old Thingummytight. You're thinking of——

HORACE : Never could tell 'em apart.

TOM : They were as like as two what-you-may-call-its.

HORACE : One had hard luck. Lost his——

TOM : Never the same man again. Well—nice to talk about old times. Call in again some day.

HORACE : I suppose I'd always find you in the how-do-you-do?

TOM : Yes, with my back to the you-know-what.

Such interruptions did not hinder the general progress of the spa. They had the luck to find a geyser, which, as

Sam Scram put it, "shot a shower of spray sky-high every seven seconds, spreading the smell of sulphur so strongly that it succeeded in sending the surrounding spectators semi-conscious."

In the middle of May there was more big news from the war fronts. All organised resistance ceased in North Africa, and General Von Arnim was a prisoner. Mr. Churchill was in Washington, and everywhere was the same rumour—a correct rumour for once—"They're fixing up the Second Front."

Tommy's topical references always got a big hand, and he saw to it that there was one right in his introductory greeting on May 13th. "Hello, folks!" he said. "Sorry I'm late. I wanted to see Winston Churchill. Hitler said he'd be in Cairo, so I went to Washington and there he was."

On the following week Tommy promised that he would provide his listeners with something really sensational. "I've just lined up General von Barnum," he said. "Later on in the programme he's going to appear in the great water spectacle entitled 'Pots Dam' thing after another'." Needless to say he didn't appear, but listeners were delighted to have return visits from two characters who had quickly become popular—Comical Chris (Bill Stephens), full of the corniest gags in the book, and Walter Wetwhite who did imitations. Both characters were so bad that listeners seemed to think them very good. I noticed, when refreshing my memory about the programme broadcast on June 10th that someone had written on the prompt copy that the show gained eighty-four laughs. Quality of the gags apart, it would not gain so many if the recording were to be broadcast now, for this show seemed to be particularly rich in highly topical remarks.

There is, for instance, Tommy's mysterious statement on the 'phone to Funf: "You got away from Tunis? Sam, ring up Churchill and tell him to make it 639." This was a reference to Mr. Churchill's "brighter and solid prospects" in a statement on the war situation in the House of Commons, during which he mentioned that only 638 of the enemy managed to escape by air from Tunisia after the capitulation.

And there was Tommy's remark that "The Fuehrer has a slight cold through paddling in the Ruhr Valley." This referred to the famous dam-busting raid by Wing-Commander Gibson, for which he was awarded the V.C. "I'll just get Pantelleria on the 'phone," was a gag on the Mussolini's island fortress then being subject to raids by air and sea day after day and night after night.

Bill Stephens, who had replaced Clarence Wright when the latter went out on a road show, had by this time made Comical Chris a well-known character. He also created the photographer with his "Smile, please" catch phrase, and another feature of this series was the musical interludes with Peter Akister and the Jazz Ticulators. Charlie Shadwell was now wise-cracking and conducting the special arrangements which had now become an important part of the show. These musical numbers were more than just a fill-up or contrast to the dialogue, and we were honoured by having a special arrangement of "What Shall We Do with a Drunken Sailor?" written for the show by the late Doctor Victor Hely-Hutchinson.

Tommy's Spa passed through innumerable adventures and vicissitudes. It became a holiday camp, was taken over by the B.B.C., changed into an hotel, and even had a zoo and circus visit it. Then came the final show on August 5th, 1943, the day the Eighth Army captured Catania and Marshal Stalin announced another big advance. Beside these great events perhaps the ITMA occasion is of rather minor significance. Yet it seemed to delight the listeners, judging from the avalanche of congratulations we had—including many from the lads in Sicily. The programme had reached its century.

"Something wonderful's happened," said Sam Scram. But Tommy knew he didn't mean the one hundredth broadcast. "I know," he replied. "They've got a room ready for him in the Isle of Man." Mussolini had resigned, and the Fascist regime in Italy was over.

The long series of summer broadcasts had been something of a strain for everyone. The show had by this time become so intricate that it required a minimum of six hours' rehearsal, and this was merely the culmination of a whole series of conferences, discussions and sectional rehearsals. ITMA had become a full-time job, despite the suggestions of well-meaning friends that Tommy was very lucky "only to have to do half an hour's work a week."

As well as snatching a week or so's vacation, we also received orders to return to London, for the danger of invasion had been officially regarded as passed. Church bells were ringing again—and they merely meant that it was time for evensong, not that paratroopers were landing. The B.B.C. had taken over the Criterion Theatre in Piccadilly Circus, and by building the stage out over the first two or three rows of the stalls and adding the usual paraphernalia of a broadcasting studio we had a very fine place in which to work. There was still, however, room for only a comparatively small audience, for the circle and boxes were used as rest rooms and sleeping places for the engineers, spotters, and so forth, whose work kept them on duty in the small hours of the morning when they could not get home.

Tommy was going to miss his weekly visits to Bangor where he had made many friends. There was also the sad fact that Jack Train would not be with the show when it opened in October. Jack had been unwell for some time, and by the end of the summer there were very definite doctor's orders that he must rest for many months. After ITMA's one-hundredth performance at the Grand Theatre, Llandudno, he was sent to a Sanatorium in North Wales, where he remained for over a year. One artiste and one good friend had left the ITMA company for a time—and with him went at least half a dozen characters, headed by his fruity, bibulous Colonel, probably the best-loved character in ITMA at that time next to Tommy himself.

The new caste supporting Tommy was Horace Percival, Fred Yule, Dorothy Summers, Sydney Keith, Dino Galvani, Bill Stephens, Bryan Herbert and Jean Capra. There were some new voices, therefore, demanding new characters. Jean Capra was a discovery of our own. She came for an audition and she impressed Tommy as that rare person—the born microphone actress. Francis and I agreed with his enthusiasm about her ability, though we were cynical enough to believe that she could not be as good all the time as she was at that audition. Time was going to prove us wrong.

Jean made her *debut* in the first programme as the daughter of Percy (Lo and Be'old) Pintable, played by Horace Percival. Her name was Effie. She introduced herself as " seventeen and never been out with an American." She was cheeky, cocky, and a very useful verbal adversary for Tom, now busily organising a fun-fair, " so that people did not get bored when peace broke out."

Jean's appearance was followed by the arrival of Sam's brother Butch, introduced to replace Jack Train's Lefty. This part was played by Bryan Herbert, a member of the B.B.C. Drama Repertory Company. He was a taciturn sort of chap replying to most of Tommy's questions with " Uh-uh " or " Could be," causing Tommy to remark : " I didn't really want to engage him, but he talked me into it."

Tommy rampaged through innumerable activities, finally coming to rest on a farm about Christmas time. Bryan Herbert, who was Irish by birth, brought along a pleasant character in the shape of the Marquis of Mourne, very hearty and very open-air. He also took over Jack Train's job of whispering in Japanese on the telephone, in the guise of the little man who caused Tommy to make three or four remarks that people whose minds were not nice seemed to misunderstand, but invariably brought an explanatory aside from Tommy that the man was looking for a telephone box, shooting-stick, deck chairs, or some such innocuous device. And while on Asiatic topics readers may like to recall the brief appearance of Jean Capra as the geisha girl in those audible but incomprehensible conversations which Jack Train had shared with Tommy during the previous series. No one ever knew what they were about, for Tommy's replies consisted of monosyllables.

There was also an interlude when Tommy visited the scholastic premises run by Dr. Smack. This was a Narkover type of place, and Tommy might have known what it was like from the conversation over the telephone with the Head. The invitation to Tommy to come over was interrupted by asides such as : " Let go my gown, Fawcett; don't tear my coat, Chumley; stop swinging on my braces, Banks." But this particular programme was rather notable for a brief interlude which most listeners will have forgotten. There was a rather forward young lady at the school, the daughter of the Headmaster. She was described by Tommy as the Sweetheart of the Classes. Her name was Sophie Tuckshop.

So came the New Year of 1944 . . . and with it exciting news for the cast of ITMA. Tommy was asked to entertain the Navy.

CHAPTER XVII

TOMMY VISITS THE NAVY

THE visit to Scapa Flow was one of the happiest occasions of Tommy's life. The invitation to go to the great Naval base was sent by the Admiralty in December, 1943, and, despite certain misgivings as to the wisdom of giving a show that was essentially for an unseen audience to a mass of matelots, plans were immediately put in hand to get the regular broadcast show recorded so that at least a week was left free for the visit northwards. Tommy, who had worked the Halls as far north as Aberdeen in his time, told us hair-raising stories of the cold, the gales, the rain and the sleet which we could expect. Those of us who did not know what life was like north of the border in winter-time took these stories of his with mental reservations. But we thought it might be advisable to take extra woollies. It wasn't long before we all realised that Tommy had not exaggerated.

As soon as the show on January 6th, 1944, was over we went home for a few hours' sleep, and then all met at Euston in time to catch the 10.20 a.m. naval train, H.M.S. *Jellicoe*—a special train run by the Admiralty for service personnel. The journey to Thurso took just over twenty-two hours, the longest train trip in Britain. Despite the hours we had to spend in the train the time passed quickly. The news that Tommy and the ITMA company was on board travelled rapidly through the corridors among the men returning from leave or going north for special service with the Russian convoys and North Atlantic patrols. Although we had been provided with sleepers no one got very much rest as the train climbed over the Grampians, and Tommy spent hour after hour in different carriages giving entertainment *ad lib*. It was an outstanding characteristic of Tommy's that he was bubbling with fun at an hour of the morning when most people are at their grumpiest. He was always an early riser and wide awake at that. Travelling often with him as I did, I had often heard him maintain a flow of fun from dawn until dusk. With brief intervals for a doze or a game of poker, the fun would continue on and, although I had heard it all before, I still enjoyed it whenever the tap was turned on. It was obvious from the remarks of these men that the Admiralty's idea of asking the ITMA company to travel to Scapa Flow was a good one. The men had a feeling that they were rather left out of things up there. The focus of public attention was on other theatres of war, and it was extremely difficult to provide adequate entertainment for the men who were stationed in this austere and out-of-the-way region.

When we left the train at Thurso to have breakfast in the Royal Hotel, the sub-Arctic weather hit us with a vengeance, but after a couple of hours for rest we went along the quayside to embark on the transport which plied between the mainland and the islands. Although the crossing is fairly narrow the meeting place of the Atlantic and the North Sea is hardly the zone for a quiet sail even in summer time. On a blustery morning in January it could usually be relied on to do its worst. However, on this morning it behaved itself and no one provided any opportunities for gags or sympathy.

Very few civilians, unless they were of the " back-room Boffin " variety, ever travelled on this ferry, for Scapa was one of the most closely guarded areas in the world, particularly after the *Royal Oak* tragedy at the beginning of the war when a U-boat got through the defences. Royal Marines patrolled everywhere, and there was a particularly hefty-looking one standing at the end of the gangplank of the ferry. Identity cards and passes had to be shown, and it was no half-hearted scrutiny that he made. The time came for Tommy to show his papers.

Now, he had for some time amused B.B.C. doormen, who were liable at intervals to start an identity card check on all studio visitors, by having a photograph of himself disguised as Hitler stuck inside his card. He had forgotten about this, and when he drew his card from his wallet the picture was, of course, still there. I saw that Tommy had lost a bit of his usual ebullience as he saw what had happened, particularly as the Marine did not smile but looked carefully from photo to original and back again. Finally he handed it over with a polite word of thanks, adding : " You seem to have changed a bit since that was taken, sir." Another victory for the Marines !

We were soon across the Straits and looking round the Nissen hut which had been allocated to us. We had rather expected a bit of a rest, but the Navy thought otherwise. Lieut. Kim Peacock, who was in charge of the arrangements, walked breezily in, and said : " Got everything you want ? Fine. We're due aboard the Flagship in an hour's time." And so, travel-stained and weary as we were, we were wafted aboard H.M.S. *Anson*, and Naval hospitality really started. The company was divided into parties. Tommy, Francis and myself were guests of the Chief Artificer's Mess, where a huge " high tea " awaited us ; they had also managed to scrounge some rum, and our tea was laced with liberal doses of this valuable medicine. We had just finished the last mouthful of food when we were taken on a tour of the ship, where Tommy was delighted to find that a large number of the ship's complement hailed from Liverpool. " Hey, Whacker ! " they said as he passed. No other introduction was needed. Anyone using that expression was a son of Merseyside—a scouser. We all thought this was just a visitors' tour, but not the Navy. After what seemed like several miles of 'tween-deck tunnels and hundreds of companionways, we came to a huge stretch of canvas screening, and a thousand or more chairs. " There you are, Mr. Handley," said the C.P.O., " this is the catapult deck—where you're to do your show."

" Show—now ? " we asked in unison.

" Yes, anything you like. Just go on and say anything. They'll love it."

There were over a thousand men there, as Tommy discovered when he pulled the canvas aside and peeped. He shouldn't have done it. At the first glimpse of his single eye peering rather timidly through the crack pandemonium broke out. It was, they supposed, a typical Tommy Handley way of starting a show. And he never hesitated for a moment. He walked on and started to entertain them. The show had no rhyme nor reason; the cast, who had prepared nothing in advance, did some act or other just to keep things rolling along. It was perfectly spontaneous from beginning to end—and probably one of the best the ITMA company ever did.

From that show we were taken to the Admiral's cabin,

a room about the size of a large studio (and actually a hospital when the ship went into action) where the traditional pink gins were handed round before a delightful dinner, over which the Admiral presided flanked by Mrs. Mopp and Poppy Poopah. An evening in the wardroom completed a strenuous forty hours of travel and entertaining, and we were all exhausted when we arrived back at our ENSA hut at midnight.

On the following morning, despite the Arctic blizzard that was blowing, Tommy and the whole Company set out for Lyness to give two shows in the cinema there while I was left in the freezing hut by a smoking fire to write the script. The ever-faithful Teenie Goss was there to type it, and as she had already made friends with the officers of a near-by Ack-Ack Battery she had it duplicated as well. She didn't have to walk to the Battery Offices—she just stood still and the wind blew her there. I felt decidedly ill and lay down at intervals, but somehow the script was finished and all ready for inspection, discussion and further cogitation on the next day. It was 2 a.m. before Tommy and Francis, who were sharing the room, returned. The gale and the thick ice on the hilly road to our hut had made their journey one of undiluted terror. Undiluted also, was the hospitality of the Navy, especially of A.C.O.S., the Admiral Commanding Orkney and Shetlands, Sir Julian Welles, who had entertained the Company at his official residence ashore.

The next day the fire petered out altogether, and so, wearing every available woolly, gloves, overcoats and scarves, we sat all day polishing and pondering over the script. We had a mass of material to choose from, for the Navy had proved rich in the sort of folklore which made ideal ITMA copy. Unfortunately a lot of it would have been unintelligible to radio audiences, and a lot more of it unacceptable to the B.B.C. censors. Tommy was full of breezy ideas—the sort which made Francis laugh a lot before he said " No." But there was one delightful line in the final programme which was a good example of his flair for a topical line. When he made the rather choppy crossing on the Sunday morning he was met by the Admiral's barge. The matelots stood nonchalantly on the bobbing deck and helped the land-lubbers to jump for it at the crucial moment when the boat was about level with the landing-stage—and not five feet above or below it. Everyone made rather a fuss about it, but the cool courtesy of the Navy ignored their clumsiness. As Tommy stumbled down the companion way, gripping, like us, everything in sight to prevent himself falling, an immaculate Flag Officer stood watching in the little cabin with a glass in his hand. " Gin, sir ? " he asked.

" Lumme," said Tommy breathlessly, " an Admiral's launch with a Gin Turret ! " This line in the script was destined to raise one of the biggest laughs.

The big show was given in the cinema on Flotta to an audience of sailors who had all just come out of action. The Naval men were off ships which had been escorting a Russian convoy, and the airmen belonged mostly to Coastal Command and the Fleet Air Arm, who had the job of searching out the U-boat nests on the Norwegian coasts. The final choice was decided by ballot. It was bitterly cold in the hall—the brass instruments were out of tune and the strings of the violins broke through it. But these little things didn't matter. The show got a tremendous reception, and is now regarded by the B.B.C. light entertainment chiefs as a classic. It has been re-broadcast on several occasions, and is played as part of the instructional courses at the B.B.C. staff college. Good as that show was the repeat given an hour later was even better. It was given after the NAAFI wet canteen had been open for some time, and overran its time by eight minutes through the sheer inability of the cast to get on with the dialogue, so great was the laughter and applause. This show was also recorded but the B.B.C. considered it too noisy for general broadcasting purposes, so it has never been heard over the air.

After giving many shows ashore and afloat on Depot ships, Aircraft Carriers, Repair Ships, and so on, we left by drifter for the island of Pomona to entertain the Fleet Air Arm and R.A.F. stationed there and in Caithness. Here the weather was warm and the reception still warmer. Three shows a day was our average, interspersed with every possible form of hospitality. From the Fleet Air Arm Station at Twatt we were flown back to Thurso in five Walruses. Tommy was superstitious about flying, having once been told that he would meet his death in a flying accident, but the Walrus, though old and slow, was a notoriously safe kite, and he enjoyed it—after landing. At the R.A.F. Station a final show was given, and so back to London by train. The visit to the Navy, the broadcast from Scapa, had proved one of the high-lights in Tommy's career. From now on, for the next five years—he was to be in constant demand. He had reached the top—he must stay there.

CHAPTER XVIII

THE OTHER SERVICES

THE success of the Navy show had started the ball rolling with the other services, and early in February we were ready with a show for the R.A.F. Francis and I had spent a day at Hornchurch, the 11 Group Fighter Station near Dagenham, picking up the gen. Hornchurch was familiar to me. I had been there with the N.Z.E.F. in 1916, at the New Zealand Convalescent Hospital, Grey Towers, and had had my first flight from that air-field.

To prepare the way for this special show we got the idea of turning Much Fiddling Manor and its farmlands into an aerodrome. This was as well, for the man from the Air Ministry arrived about the same time to commandeer the place. The interview was interrupted by a 'phone conversation which seemed to delight a public which had been getting just a little impatient with Tommy over a certain Peter Geekie. This chap was a very old friend of Tommy's. He had stored the name in his memory for more than thirty years, the earliest of his collection of queer and yet authentic characters. The name Peter Geekie he had seen on the brass plate of an office in Liverpool's dockland when he was an office boy with the toy firm. There had been others in the years that followed (such as the off-licence which he thought was owned by William IV, but was merely the jug and bottle department of the William the Fourth

Inn, and so got banished from the list when this was discovered). But none matched up to Peter Geekie in Tommy's estimation. Why this should be, I frankly don't know. It did not seem to others such an unusual name (there are two Geekies in the London telephone directory to-day, plenty more in the provinces, and thousands in Scotland), but Tommy had continually hoped for an excuse to use it. He just introduced the name for no reason at all, and I wrote him into the script each week. The man was the Great Unknown of the programmes, blamed for everything, praised for everything, used for every senseless telephone call. The nonsense, which had frankly seemed to us a little bit too reasonless even for ITMA, had caught on in a big way. Schoolmasters had learned that to enquire " Who left the door open ? " would bring only one answer— " Peter Geekie." In the operations rooms of the R.A.F. and the Royal Observer Corps the tracks of aircraft which later proved to be non-existent were often logged as the work of Peter Geekie. Peter Geekie left lights on, taps running, knocked at doors and ran. He had become a national nuisance—and a national mystery. He was the legitimate successor to Funf.

On February 3rd listeners heard Tommy's 'phone ring.

" Hello ! " he said.

" Is that yon sleekit, creepit gowk, Tommy Handley ? " a voice demanded.

" Aye," said Tommy.

" The yin that's speirin' about ma brither's bairn ? "

" Aye (what's he talking about ?). Who's speaking, please ? "

This looked like it. But it wasn't.

" Andra' Geekie, Peter Geekie's uncle. Ye've gi'en

the laddie a rare opinion o' himself. His heed's aw' swellin'. He's gangin' roond the toon like a dug wi' twa tails. He's aw puffit oot. We Geekie's are comin' to London tae stop aw' this bletherin'."

But no one ever met Peter himself, although a name-sake—a fruiterer in Edinburgh—frequently visited Tommy in London.

Then came the R.A.F. edition. It was broadcast on February 17th with an all-airmen and air-women audience. As soon as it was over we started outlining the plan for the third special show, for the Army.

There was no doubt that the Air Force edition had not gone over with such a bang as the Navy show, and we felt certain that the reason for this was that the audience at the Criterion Theatre were very conscious that they were in a broadcasting studio. There is a lot of nonsense talked by some people of the fact that laughter, clapping and general audience reaction is carefully rehearsed beforehand, and the unfortunates who accept free tickets for these events are drilled like a regiment of guardsmen, shrieking with laughter when a stage-hand holds up a card marked LAUGH and clapping like mad when he changes it to APPLAUSE. Equally foolish is the theory that people try to make a noise so that they can enquire of their listening families later : " Did you hear me laugh after the third joke of the second turn ? " There is, however, a lot of truth that a studio audience does not act as naturally as it would in an ordinary theatre, unless they are given a little warming chat first (which is what I used to do before all the ITMA shows in later years). This was what was wrong with the " colour " of the R.A.F. edition. We decided we would not make that mistake in the case of the Army, and so we went down in a furniture

van to the Garrison Theatre, Woolwich, to give it—
where there would be no inhibitions and the lads and
lassies in khaki could let themselves go with all
the fervour of the men of Scapa Flow if they felt
inclined.

Thus it was that, on April 13th, with machine-guns
cracking and guns booming, the Army edition of ITMA
went on the air. Paula Green was not in this show,
for she had left for an ENSA tour overseas, and Jack
Cooper had the singing to do in her stead. We still
needed another girl for the speaking parts. We chose
Diana Morrison, who was destined to remain with us
for five years. She was a great artist from the start;
she gave Tommy confidence, was a brilliant character
actress and experienced broadcaster. On this occasion
there was, of course, no Miss Hotchkiss. Diana played
the part of Aunt Sally, a charming old girl who continually worried about her nephew Tommy-wommy.
She was completely happy lecturing the dear boys on
Shakespeare and old English dances until, as she explained, they had to leave for their wallop, " a kind of
cocoa."

Squire Handley continued with his bizarre activities
until the thirty-sixth show of this series. Much had
happened since its first edition in October, 1943. Then
Mr. Churchill had said : " The Second Front, which
already exists potentially and which is rapidly gathering
weight has not been engaged, but it is here."

And on that June morning when I was on my way to
the studio for rehearsal, I met Tommy, who told me,
and we switched on the eight o'clock news. " Allied
Forces landed on the beaches of Normandy."

It was D Day.

A new series was booked for September, and it seemed

only reasonable that the three fighting services having been duly given special programmes, war industry might like the same gesture. So off we went to the great tank and army vehicle factory of Wolseley Motors at Birmingham. Jack Train was back with us, fit and well ; Paula Green had returned from ENSA ; and we had the augmented Midland Light Orchestra providing the musical background.

It looked quite a rosy sort of plan, but on the train back from Birmingham Tommy looked across at me and said, " Well, that's one way to make our hats fit again if we needed it. That show was a flop." Both Francis and I had to agree with him that things could have been better. There was that indefinable something missing from the laughter and the applause, but we did not think that it had been quite as bad as Tommy suggested. In fact, a Movietone News Reel taken at the time rather supports this. However, when we started looking through the ITMA postbag it was obvious that Tommy's knowledge of audience reaction had been right. There were not so many letters as usual.

What had gone wrong ? There had been no hitches despite the inevitable first show nerves at the first of a new series. " I'll tell you what it is," said Tommy. " We've built up a studio show and we've been trying to make it a visual show. It can't be done. I know that the Services liked it, but that was different. There we could introduce gags about their lives and environment which every one of them knew about because it was part of his existence. But gags about industrial production don't fit so easily. Something funny about the foreman in one works won't amuse the people at another plant."

Of course, Tommy was right. From that time onwards ITMA was never performed outside a studio.

However, to show that there were some memorable moments in this first broadcast of the new series, I should like to quote one or two extracts. There was, for instance, this example of dialogue which was later to become a regular feature :

" Hello there, Tommy bach—there's welcome you are . . ." said a voice.

And Tommy replied : " It's the patriotic conductor, hip-hip-hooray Jenkins—conduct something for me—you've got your stick in your hand."

" That's not a stick ; that's me," said Charlie Shadwell.

And so " for the first time on any programme," Tommy's two favourite conductors appeared together. The reason was, of course, that as we were in the Midlands we were using Rae Jenkins' Orchestra, and the two conductors shared the honours of conducting. Tommy made a note that Rae was almost incapable of reading more than six words of script without stumbling, and he told me that if only Rae could practise hard enough to retain that inability it might one day make a very good gag sequence for the show. Later events were to prove how right he was.

The theme of the first programme had been Tommy's discovery of a Plan. As he expressed it, it was high time that we started preparing for peace—a reasonable suggestion in view of the way the Guards Brigade had swept along the Channel coast and into Belgium while the Americans, headed by General Patton, were rushing for the borders of Germany farther south. There was, at this time, not unreasonable talk that the war would be over by Christmas.

In the second programme the Plan did not progress very much, for Tommy was too busy engaging staff. He was getting along quite gaily when the door opened and there rang out some words which were to terrorise Tommy's life and delight his listeners.

"Mr. Handley! Mr. Handley! Mr. Handley!" she said.

"Yes, yes, yes," replied Tommy. "Oh, sorry, are you my new secretary? What a clock!"

"Hotchkiss is the name. Have you anything to dictate? I'll give you a week's trial; if I find you steady, sober and reliable, I'll stay."

It looked as if Tommy's happy days were over. When Paula Green dropped in for her usual flirtation Miss Hotchkiss said very firmly: "I do not encourage young women in office hours." But the motive, we may be sure, was then merely one of efficiency. Jealousy had still to raise its ugly head and cause unmaidenly thrills in her manly chest. She was a character who caught on immediately—and delighted the world.

The term "world" is used advisedly. The ITMA audience was now spread over two hemispheres. On Thursday it was broadcast on the Home Service, on Sundays and Wednesdays on the General Forces Programme, on Wednesday nights on the General Overseas Service, on Mondays on the red network of the Pacific Service, and on Monday nights and on Tuesday mornings on the North American Service: a little later the African Service was included as well. Tommy could justly claim to be a comedian with the largest audience ever known.

Many of the old favourites were still in the programme. The Colonel was drinking his way in and out of the office, Paula was flirting before each song, and Mrs.

Mopp was bringing her gifts. It was in the second programme that Tommy achieved what probably stands as a record length for his good-bye abbreviation. It was N.K.A.B.T.Y.S.I.R.W.U.—"Never kiss a baby till you're sure it's right way up."

During the programmes up to Christmas-time Tom was busy on his election campaign as a candidate for Parliament. His rival was the notorious Peter Geekie, who never got to the hustings. There were, of course, innumerable interruptions to the main story, and one of the inconsequential ones which listeners seemed to like very much was the interview which went like this :

FRED YULE : Excuse me—but have you got a want ?
TOM : Oh, I've lots of wants. What kind of want do you want ?
FRED YULE : A long want.
TOM : I hope this is long enough——
FRED YULE : The very thing—made of felt too—that's splendid.
TOM : Do you want me to fill it ?
FRED YULE : No thanks—I can manage.

Tommy explained that here was a man who went round filling a long-felt want.

And there was Horace Percival's interminable conundrums which Tommy, with perfect *savoir faire*, always answered. This is a typical one, broadcast on Boxing Day, 1944 :

HORACE : There was a Christmas party in Hollywood— all the stars were there—Charlie Chaplin wore a bowler hat. Gary Cooper wore a sombrero, Betty Grable wore tights and Bette Davis wore a smile—Dorothy Lamour came in late, she didn't wear a hat—she didn't wear a coat

—she didn't wear riding breeches—what did she wear?

There's no need to give Tommy's reply. Anyway, Horace confirmed it with : " S'right."

The old catch phrases had been in use for some time, and the listeners found something new to their liking in the conversations of Mark Time, played by Jack Train. This hoary old reprobate could never satisfy Tom about anything, for before committing himself he always warned : " I'll have to ask me dad."

In the New Year the Colonel caused a sensation by going teetotal. He advised Tommy to eschew alcohol as well. " Handley," he pointed out, " if you went teetotal you wouldn't see that pink rat on the table." Tommy observed that the Colonel's resolution had resulted in all the publicans going about with their trousers at half-mast.

In this programme, the first of 1945, Tommy was persuaded by Sam Scram to go into a nursing home for publicity reasons.

Paula and Jean, in the guise of two nurses, held the following conversation :

PAULA : Did you hear who's coming in as a patient, ducks? You'll never believe it. You won't really.
JEAN : Oh, go on, tell me.
PAULA : Well, promise you won't tell. It's——
        (*She whispers.*)
JEAN : Go on, him that's on the wireless? Let's make him an apple-pie bed.

In actual fact the patient was to be Francis Worsley. He had spinal trouble and was ordered into hospital, where, incidentally, he remained for seven months. It was a real crisis for ITMA. Finally, it was agreed that he could produce the show from his bed, and the headquarters of ITMA were transferred to the private ward of the hospital, and Ronnie Waldman took over the show on the floor.

Tommy's trip to hospital was as hilarious as Francis's was tedious, but it had a strange sequel. While the repeats of the January 18th broadcast were transmitting dialogue explaining that he had been thrown out of hospital on his ear, Tommy was actually ill in bed. He was down with 'flu, and for the first time in his life missed an ITMA broadcast. As already mentioned, the Navy show of the previous winter was transmitted instead of the normal programme.

The announcement which preceded this, referring to Tommy's absence through illness, brought a tremendous number of letters and 'phone calls, and I think that it was a personal pleasure to millions of people when they heard the opening announcement on February 8th. It started with Fred Yule saying : " Shall I put the record on now, guv'nor ? " And the announcer replied : " No, not that record again. He's back again. He's all right again. IT'S THAT MAN AGAIN."

A newspaper, a bank, a housing scheme, a block of flats—these were some of the activities which occupied Tommy's attention during the spring and early summer of 1944. The ITMA team had a new recruit in mid-March when Ann Rich came along as a singer and as a Scots lassie—" a smashing slice of porridge," as Tommy described her.

Herr Johann Bull made one of his by now rare appearances. He came along to see Tommy on the building site of the ITMA block of flats and remarked : " I wish

a flat to engage for my greatest friendt." And Tommy
answered : " Oh him—well what flavoured carpet would
he like—raspberry ? " It was a topical question. Hitler
was busy preparing his new headquarters in his Southern
Redoubt, for both the British and American forces were
now pouring over the Rhine for the final assault on the
Reich.

But it is notable that this series of programmes did
not contain so many war references as those in the past.
We had thought that the news was good enough in itself.
Wise-cracks and witticisms were not needed to raise the
morale of the people. The war in Europe was almost
over. There was, however, one little sequence in the
programme on April 5th which will help to refresh the
memory of those good news-filled days. Horace Percival
had a topical conundrum which went like this : " One
hundred thousand Germans were caught in the Ruhr,
another hundred thousand are surrounded in Holland,
Montgomery's on one side, Bradley's on the other,
Patton's getting round in front, Dempsey's getting round
behind—what does Hitler say to Himmler ? "

Tommy was three weeks too early with his answer :
" Shut up the shutters and sit in the shop."

But the time inevitably came for V-ITMA. We had
the script ready for some time, and Francis, who had
happily been released from hospital in time to produce
the show personally, asked that it should be a celebration
marked particularly by Tommy himself. He would be
allowed to *ad lib.* if he wanted ; he could really let
himself go. We brought in characters who had not
appeared for some time—the Mer, the Town Treasurer,
and other friends from Foaming-at-the-Mouth.

Tommy had his Victory speech all ready, " though "
(as he said) " he needed a cigar and a new set of victory

G

fingers before he could give it." Charlie Shadwell had
a special arrangement of "Happy Days Are Here
Again," and later Tommy revived one of his old favourites, "The Man with the Big Cigar," but now the words
were new :

"We're glad we walked behind the man who smoked the big
    cigar.
        Tra-la-la-la. Tra-la-la-la. Tra-la-la-la-la-la.
We'd follow the man whose master plan has carried us through
    the war.
        Tra-la-la-la. Tra-la-la-la. Tra-la-la-la-la-la.
One sniff of the Old Havana—we'd follow him right to Fugi-
    Yama.
We'd follow him most anywhere, the man with the big cigar,
        Tra-la-la-la. Tra-la-la-la. Tra-la-la-la-la-la."

It was a parody of a song Tommy recalled from his
early visits to the Isle of Man concert parties.

There were two more broadcasts after the V-ITMA
show. The final one of the series was broadcast on
June 14th. Tommy explained that he had joined the
Secret Service which would necessitate his absence for
some weeks, but listeners were reassured with the fade-
out chorus which promised that : " Like the frost and
the fog he'd come back."

Another thirty-nine shows were over. They had begun
with the staccato noise of doodlebugs over London as
we went to rehearsals ; they had continued with the
roar of the " gas mains " exploding (how we wished
that we could have used some gags on that code description of the early V2's) ; and they had ended with Europe
liberated. We wondered, as we said good-bye at a little
party after the show, whether the September series
would be broadcast for a nation completely at peace
or still at war in the East. The tremendous area over-run

by the Japanese seemed to make this happy possibility too optimistic for realisation, and Tommy had agreed with me that his Secret Service activities would allow us to move his adventures to the Pacific. But Tommy's spies were as inefficient as any ITMA undercover agent. They had failed to discover the existence of the atom bomb.

CHAPTER XIX

TOMMY IN PEACETIME

IN those first weeks of peace we had some serious thinking to do about Tommy's future activities in ITMA programmes. For more than 170 performances basically the same line-up of characters had strutted and fretted their half-hour before the microphone. It was true that their numbers had increased almost every month, but anyone who had missed every show after those broadcasts in the Bristol days would have recognised the structure as the same. Furthermore, it was fairly certain that listeners who hadn't missed many editions were not tired—yet. But it's a good rule in show business to "leave off when they're calling for more," and with mixed feelings we decided that this should be done with ITMA.

I well remember how depressed Tommy was about it all—his feelings were mingled between a realisation of the need to get some freshness into the picture and regret at parting with old friends. And so we decided that characters such as Mrs. Mopp, Signor So-So, the Diver, Sam Scram, and a host of others, would not appear in the new series. It meant the end of a record innings by a perfect team, and we had no illusions that we could easily find another one as good, even if it might have the quality of novelty and contrast. But the fates were kind, and before long there was a new ITMA company which, we were told, was administering the mixture as before, but with a new and maybe more piquant taste.

That was that. Next came the need to change the scene. The peace was too young for us to be sure of a topical theme which would remain fresh over thirty-nine weeks. And the rather vague and disconnected adventures which had sufficed in the previous series were, we decided, not really good enough for a show which depended to a great extent on continuity of action by the same characters, even if we were starting a new chapter.

" Let's invent an undiscovered island of our own," I said. " It ought to be a Handley's Lilliput, a Tommy's Never-never-land, an ITMA Utopia."

" Yes," said the best-known voice on the radio. " Tomtopia."

And it was.

The new show opened on September 20th with seven separate transmissions, and Tommy's introductory greeting : " It's turned out peace again," was interrupted by a newcomer to the cast, Carleton Hobbs (who had started broadcasting as early as Tommy himself) as the Toastmaster. It was a small rôle compared with Major Munday, Curly Kale and the " Ain't it a shame ? " man which he created in later programmes. Clarence Wright was back with the show (" Good morning, nice day "), and of course the Colonel was cadging drinks as usual.

The programme proceeded in quite a leisurely manner until the last quarter of an hour when listeners were given a clue of the future developments. The Toastmaster came in and said : " Mr. Handley, His Majesty's Government whom I represent have deputed me to request you to leave this realm immediately. A great honour has been conferred on you. You have been appointed Governor of a new island recently discovered."

There were preparations, of course—and interruptions. A charming one came from Tommy's old nurse, played by Mary O'Farrell, a lady with similar tastes to the Colonel's and a wealth of earthy reminiscences of bottles, talcum powder and smackings. And then there was Lind Joyce making her *debut* with " I want the Waiter," Poppy Poopah and her father (the latter portrayed by Hugh Morton) and Mark Time. Tommy quite rightly felt that he had at least the nucleus of an entourage. More bizarre characters appeared during the four weeks' voyage to the island. There was the arch Lady Sonely —" You naughty man, I'd know you anywhere. You will help with the ship's concert, won't you ? " And there was Sam Fairfechan (Hugh Morton), who first said what he ought, and said what he thought immediately afterwards. He was the ship's engineer on the voyage. Tommy met him in the engine-room. " Come down by all means—I have taken the ladder away," said Sam. " Full steam ahead we are going—backwards," he added as he explained the workings of the ship. He was perfectly capable in his job too. " I'm a qualified engineer ; I know all about engines. I haven't the slightest no-TION."

Another member of the ship's queer complement was George Gorge, the dining-room stowaway. His breakfast whetted the appetites of a Britain rapidly learning that the sudden cessation of Lease-Lend was going to keep Austerity to the forefront for a long time to come. He itemised the dishes to Tommy : " I've had six plates of porridge, a pork chop, three plates of fat bacon and fried eggs, lashings of waffles and maple syrup, and a gallon of coffee. Lovely grub ! Lovely grub ! "

But all Tommy said was : " What—no toast and marmalade ? "

This food was prepared by Kurly Kale. It made him sick to think of it. He hated his job, but loved his repertoire of hoary old stories told in a flat monotone like this :

" A man was eating in a restaurant one day and the next day another man said ' what was the ladle I saw you eating with last night ? ' and the first man replied ' that was no ladle that was my knife.' Do you like that ? " He had a gag book full of chestnuts of a similar age—sufficient to last for several programmes. Two cabin boys were also very much to the fore, to Tommy's embarrassment. They were played by Lind Joyce and Jean Capra.

The long voyage neared its end by October 25th, and Tommy viewed the future with some misgivings. He had heard that the last ENSA company to visit the Island had gone down well. " The population simply ate 'em."

But it was not so bad. Big Chief Bigga Banga jabbered his welcome, and Major Munday explained that he had been on the island since the war (" The Queen never sent my passage money "). And right at the end of this programme came a couple of words : " Mister Handley." Miss Hotchkiss was on the quayside waiting to greet her idol with the feet of clay. She got a tremendous reception from the studio audience—as she had from us at the rehearsal which she attended rather against the wishes of her doctor. For Diana had been ill and had missed the boat to Tomtopia. We were very glad that by a wave of the radio wand we could whirl her out to the island in time to greet the boss.

In the following show Tommy was officially installed

as the Governor of Tomtopia. His official liaison with
the chief was simplified by platonic liaison with the
chief's daughter Banjoleo, who had a smattering of
English and was, in Tommy's view, a " smashing portion
of passion fruit, well worth a second helping." To
Tommy's infinite pleasure she brought an invitation
from her father to a dinner—undress optional.

Tommy, of course, gave a reception in return, and
among the guests were Major Munday and his daughter
Naieve (Jean Capra). Her first talk with the Governor
was typical of them all.

TOM : Would you like to do the foxtrot with me ?
JEAN : Foxtrot. What is that ?
TOM : Well, a man puts his arm round a girl, stands on
her feet, rests his head on her shoulders and
talks through her hair.

In contrast to this simplicity there was the surprising
sophistication of Wamba M'Boojah (Hugh Morton), the
ebony chief with the advantages of a public school
education ; " I say, Handley old man," he complained
one day ; "this is really a bit thick. A native constable
has just been through all my clothes."

For an unknown island Tomtopia was getting pretty
full. Just before Christmas, 1945, Stella Stalls turned
up with her dramatic company, quoting Shakespeare
and determined to bring the best in the world's drama
to the native population. And there were two Japanese
hawkers, Bowing and Scraping. They were a peace-
time version of Ali-Oop, and based on Tommy's Chinese
pirate character he had played just after the first world
war when the undergraduates at Cambridge wrecked
the show by inserting " l's " into Tommy's dialogue.
Bowing and Scraping also did this in every remark.

One very popular sequence in this series was the reminiscent chat each week between the Colonel and the Major. This was an example, broadcast in January just after gold had been discovered in a remote corner of Tomtopia.

JACK TRAIN :	This gold rush's dangerous, Munday. I hope you carry a gun. I always have one with me.
TOM :	Have one with you, Colonel ? I'll have a large gin and Jumbo.
CARLETON HOBBS and JACK :	Silence, civilian !
TOM :	Quiet, conscript !
CARLETON :	I say, Chinstrap, my nephew, Montgomery Munday, once drank a toast to his Colonel's daughter out of her slipper and passed out——
TOM :	What was her size in shoes ? Fourteen and a half ?
CARLETON :	She was engaged to Figgy Fitzwallaby.
JACK :	Poor old Figgy. I sat next to him the night he smeared the General's face with mayonnaise and tried to shave him with a fish knife. Definitely dirty what ?
TOM :	Oh, I don't know. I sat next to Jimmy Wilde at dinner the other night—he jumped into the serviette ring, went three rounds with a black pudding, gave the steak pie a kidney punch and feinted into the trifle. Any questions ?
JACK :	By the way, Munday. Do you know that a submarine can now go to America and back without coming to the surface ?
CARLETON :	Tchah ! You shouldn't believe everything you read in Jules Verne.

Things were really cracking in Tomtopia by February. There was a railway and a railway refreshment room. Tommy went round to see it. " No cups outside ! " came the order between the hiss of steam from the tea and cocoa urns. Ruby Rockcake was on duty.

The two hundredth edition of ITMA was broadcast on February 21st. There were some congratulatory messages, or at least Tom purported to be reading them from authentic telegrams. For instance : " Congratulations. For the two hundredth time I have not heard you—Dr. Joad." Tommy's reply was : " Thanks for your good wishes—always delighted to hear from a brother comic."

Even the B.B.C. was supposed to have sent one. " We take back all we said about your programme. Have found the kipper nailed under the listening room table."

But the general celebrations of the anniversary were marred by bad news. Whitehall, disturbed by the reports of the goings-on in Tomtopia, were sending a Commission to investigate the situation. The members were Lord Slough of Despond, Sir Alexander Palace, the Hon. Mrs. de Point, and a Scotsman—Mr. Soccyhall.

At last came June 13th—and the final programme of the 1945–46 series. It coincided with the Victory celebrations in London and so, of course, Tomtopia had a Victory procession too. At the head was the Tomtopian Home Guard, then swinging along in their grass kilts the Girl Guides, led by Harriet Hotchkiss. The town band came next, the sons of toil, the land girls, and the Colonel and the Major representing the veterans (with a lorry load of empties bringing up the rear). And so, with Rae Jenkins playing him out, the ninth series was over.

Rae Jenkins had succeeded the most insulted musician in the world—Charles Shadwell, whose thinness had been the butt of Tommy's humour since 1941. Charles had left the B.B.C. to tour with his own orchestra.

Just before the ITMA cast broke up for the summer season, Tommy and the rest of us were honoured with one of the most unusual gestures it can ever have been the lot of a comedy outfit to receive. An admirer, Colin Hurry, arranged a Tomtopian lunch. It was held at the Connaught Rooms, London, on June 7th, 1946. The rooms had been wonderfully decorated to give atmosphere. Stuffed tigers loomed out of fake palm trees, snakes writhed up the pillars, and the chair was taken by a large and fortunately dead ape. The chief item on the wine list was Jungle Juice. The menu, designed by Mendoza, had caricatures of all the cast and the meal, consisting of interminable courses worthy of the finest chefs of France, had everything neatly deleted with the word " off " alongside. The only item on the whole card left " on " was " café." And even this had a note : " No lait."

Tommy was, of course, delighted with the idea, but neither he nor any of the rest of us who were guests had any conception of what was to follow the luncheon. We found that our host had really taken the fictional Government Commission literally, and the famous people who had, we thought, just come along as distinguished and unexpected fans of the programme went into committee to report their findings. A senior civil servant with a lifetime of experience in Colonial administration ripped the official policy of Governor Handley to shreds, programme by programme ; a lawyer found the legal and judiciary system wanting ; a sociologist was alarmed at the position of women in the island, quoting Naieve's abysmal ignorance of the facts of life as damning evidence of the lack of culture and education.

Our heads were bloody at the end of it. We were also tremendously impressed with the really wonderful idea these new-found friends of ours had had. Francis made arrangements to have the tribunal's proceedings re-created for a broadcast programme, and so Tomtopia found official or near-official recognition.

CHAPTER XX

TOM MARCHES ON

IN the autumn of 1946 the tenth series of ITMA opened with Governor Handley still on extended leave from his Tomtopian island. Listeners soon learned that, according to the police, his address was now Castle Weehouse, Dire Straights, Loch Tynn, Scotland, and here some of his stalwarts, headed by the persistent Hotch, followed him.

Jean Capra had left the cast for a more important rôle as a real-life mother for the second time, and partly to make up for her absence Francis had engaged Molly Weir, a Scots girl who played the part of Tattie Mackintosh in this series. It was, as a matter of fact, the intriguing Scottish accent of this lassie at an audition during the summer which gave us the idea of setting the new series in a locale North of the Tweed. And just for contrast, we were also delighted to have the most soul-searing Cockney voice on record—that of Joan (Mona Lott) Harben. She was heard at the same audition as Molly, and this can probably go on record as the most fruitful audition we ever held.

Masculine additions to the cast included Deryck Guyler, who hailed from Wallasey, Cheshire, and knew Liverpool as well as Tommy himself. Deryck had already had some useful work to his credit as Sir Percy Palaver in the previous Tomtopia series, apart from an immense variety of serious parts in radio drama, and was in this series to create the delightful characters of Dan Dungeon the Castle Guide, Sir Short Supply and the immortal Frisby Dyke.

There was certainly the whirl of the kilts and the burr of the Scots' accent in the opening show of the series, with Tommy's Liverpudlian accent holding grimly on in the castle on the lonely moors. He was living incognito, with the name of Mungo Mucklebairn, and the locals' opinion of him was best summed up by Tattie, who told Miss Hotchkiss :

" He's daft. Sits in his wee room in the wee house all day and makes me pour his porridge under the wee door. He's a' towsie and mixtie-muxtie."

Visitors were soon making the ITMA door work overtime. After a brief interview with Hotch, Frisby made his *debut* with Tommy's favourite Merseyside greeting " Hey Whacker ! " and finishing his conversation with the phrase which was to make him famous in a few weeks—" They don't never tell no one nothing these days, do they ? " Then came the deputation from Tomtopia and the public-school accent of Wamba M'Boojah (" the black man's Stewart Hibberd," as Tommy described him) with his weary-voiced protests about the Governor's refusal to return : " Handley, old man—this is utterly outrageous, but utterly ! "

Half-way through the broadcast came a new experiment for ITMA—imitations. They were made by Tony Francis, one of the cleverest men at " noises " there is. ITMA had, I think, acclimatised the public to a world of make-believe in which sound created complete characters with the barest minimum of description. An accent, a catch-phrase, and peculiar mannerism—and out of them came a person as real, we hoped, as any seen on the stage or screen. Our ambition was to extend this idea into the realm of things as well as persons. Tony gave brilliant imitations of skidding cars, trains, galloping horses, a crowded public house, as part of a story. Listeners wrote in to say how good they were; many queried whether they weren't recordings of the real thing; hundreds wanted to know more about them—but almost all felt that it was a hitch in the smooth run of the ITMA story. In brief, an experiment in sound hadn't come off, and after a few more programmes the idea was regretfully abandoned.

Sam Fairfechan brought his sister along—Pam (played by Lind Joyce). She suffered from the family failing of contradictions, explaining to Tommy that her brother had told her all about Tommy. " But I'm too young to understand—you wicked old man." She was, it was revealed, a member of the Mynorchy Male Voice Choir.

The idea of relations was contagious. Almost immediately afterwards the Colonel's nephew (Hugh Morton) made his microphone *debut*. Brigadier Dear was everything the Colonel wasn't. " Don't drink—don't smoke—must keep fit ; every morning run five miles—cold tub, rub down, physical jerks—fit as a fiddle. Youngest Brigadier in the army," he told the thunder-struck Tommy, who for once could murmur little beyond : " I wish you'd put a mute in it." Hugh was another radio artiste of vast experience who raised every character he played into a classic.

All these interruptions prevented Tommy from explaining his current ambition until almost the end of the programme ; he intended to construct a moon rocket. The heady news of atomic power had started every hare-brained inventor and imaginative scientist writing articles about his proposals in the Sunday papers. Thursday's ITMA wasn't going to be out of the swim.

In the third programme Hugh Morton introduced the twisted initial man :

" Good morning, would you care for a sninch of puff ? " he asked. " It's so good for a nold in the cose."

" I never touch it," said Tom, catching on, " it hains my stankies."

His real reason for coming proved to be that he was interested in the mip to the Troon, though he couldn't invest anything in the project, being woke to the bride.

Tommy had by this time been doing a little memory refreshing about the Brigadier, and he found to his delight that among his many friends of the old days on the stage he had often had some pretty high old times with the Brigadier's mother. It was obvious she had changed considerably with the passing years. Tommy's first memory, as recounted to the Colonel was : " Crafty Clara ? I can see her now on the night Ladysmith was relieved, chasing a masher round Piccadilly with a sausage " (" It was a stick of rhubarb," the Colonel believed).

The reminiscences were interrupted by the arrival of a possible financier of the rocket scheme—Edward Bye-gum, an industrialist of Huddersfield (played in the Priestley manner by Deryck Guyler). He was a plain man, a blunt man, but with bags of brass. To help him assess the technicalities he brought Professor Preston Pans, who explained the whole thing : " As every schoolboy knows, by proffering the parlour dome with a dimple rollered snuggle-trip, the full force of the running cost is panamaed on the frontalpiece to eliminate the catalytic wintergrill on the renegade."

Here's Wishing You Well Again. Tommy with the wounded, 1943

Tommy talks to the blinded ex-servicemen, 1943

At a Garden Fête at Hawkhurst, Kent, Tommy finds the fairies at the bottom of the garden.

With the then Mayor of Westminster, Councillor Hal Gutteridge, Tommy presents food parcels from Australia

Delegates to the African Conference in London visit *Itma*, October 7, 1948 (Tommy with Nana Sir Tsibu Darku IX, O.B.E., Omanhene of Asin Atandisu (left) and Mr. Ameri Tago of Zanzibar)

And there were always hundreds of autograph books to sign

It was only at home that he could relax

His golfing exploits ended with his touring days. He never played
after 1939

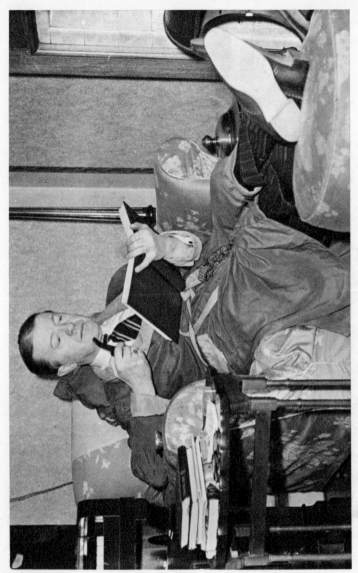

He read a lot. Latterly it was his only recreation

F. J. Standerwick

In the garden at Egham, where he rested at week-ends

West Lancashire Evening Gazette

Tommy on his last visit to Blackpool

Mona Lott made her first appearance on October 16th with the following dialogue :

JOAN HARBEN : Good morning, sir. What a shocking day. Got rheumatism that bad you wouldn't believe. What with that and my catarrh. . . . Here's your laundry.

TOM : What's this ? " Enclosed please find buttons ; shirt follows next week. *P.S.*—In future please take socks out of boots before sending." They're getting fussy. So you suffer from catarrh, do you ?

JOAN : Yes, something chronic ; makes me so deaf I can't hear myself cough.

TOM : Oh, I'll give you something to fix that.

JOAN : What—make me hear better ?

TOM : No, make you cough louder. Cheer up !

JOAN : Ah, it's all very well for you to laugh. You don't have to spend your time washing like me.

TOM : I do, but I must admit I skip the back of the neck on Thursday. I've got my hands full, anyway.

JOAN : Don't talk about hands—swelled up something enormous they have. Look at this.

TOM : It is huge. Take it along to Carrol Levis. He's always asking for a big hand for his discoveries. By the way, what's your name ?

JOAN : Mona Lott, sir.

TOM : Mona Lott. Any relation to Gordon Crier ? Off you go, and keep your pecker up.

JOAN : I always do, sir. It's being so cheerful as keeps me going.

It was a phrase to keep her going in programme after programme—the saddest, funniest character of all ITMA folklore, according to some people.

Talking about Cockneys, listeners have probably not forgotten the little stories told by " 'Ard up and 'Appy," whose life was one long saga of fortunes narrowly missed. For example, in the two hundred and twenty-second show he told Tommy about his Aunt Phœbe—" 'er wot owned two houses and had a stocking up the chimney. I used to see her regular every week. Sat for hours playing wiv her pet cat. I hoped she'd remember me in 'er will, see. And blimey she did ! She left me the cat. Cor—talk about laugh ! Ah well— 'Ard up and 'Appy, that's me."

This programme, by the way, was a farewell one for Diana Morrison. She had told us at the beginning of the series that for reasons of coming motherhood she would be following Jean some time before Christmas, and it was with regret that Tommy had to bid adieu to his much-maligned secretary (who had arranged for Thérèsa Blades to deputise for her in her absence—a rôle played by Joan Harben). By Tommy's own wish there was an armistice in their sparring at the end of the programme. Hotch was told " to shut her eyes, come closer "—and she had the kiss she had hoped for so long. She could only say one thing, and that was " Bood-gye."

" And lolly good juck," said Tommy—a wish that expressed the feelings of all the cast and her millions of fans.

Soon after this programme Tommy was ready to take off in his rocket. Jack Train came along as Luke Slippy, the American publicity man. He did a grand job of work. The whole nation avidly listened to news of the project. The rocket was fired, soared into space—and landed in Tomtopia.

Tommy did not have it all his own way on his return

to the Island. There was the opposition of Sir Percy Palaver, the mumbling bastion of the Colonial Office and his wife, which after a carefully rigged election resulted in a tie and the necessity to divide Tomtopia into zones. Probably the only person at this time who left Tommy speechless was the Joan Harben character of the woman full of good works and capable of gushing speech at a record speed in the pursuance of her aims. This is typical of her non-stop sentence in the Christmas period festivities in 1946 :

"Dear Mr. Handley—I hoped I'd find you in—we are getting up a New Year's party for the poor natives and I would so like you to come along and arrange the games. I thought we might start off with Black Man's Buff and Tropical Chairs just to get everyone mixed up and sitting on each others' laps. Then when the ice is broken we could go on to the Hokey Cokey. I'm sure they would just adore putting their left arms in and their right legs out and shaking them a little and turning themselves about. Then if I can get some apples we can play eating apples in a bowl of water if you've got a bowl. If not we shall have to use gooseberries in a slop basin, but I think it's more fun the other way round, don't you? I knew you'd agree." Her name? No one ever knew. Tommy once tried to find out, and all he heard was : "You must know me—I come in here every Thursday night to have a little chat with you."

This little chat was the longest piece of uninterrupted dialogue we ever used in ITMA with the exception of occasional speeches by Tommy himself.

Miss Hotchkiss—having presented her husband, John (In Town To-night) Ellison, with a son, Christopher— was back in late January, 1947, just in time to criticise

Tommy's six months' plan to inveigle tourists to Tom-topia. The plan went bust with a vengeance when Hotch's impatience was at last exhausted, and she took over the Tomtopian reins as Prime Minister. She faced a crisis almost immediately—shortage of ice and a breakdown of supplies on the Island. She wasn't the only statesman with troubles of that sort at that time. This programme was broadcast during the fuel crisis of February, 1947, when B.B.C. programmes were cut down and switch-offs were a rule rather than an exception. The inverted topical angle was continued when Tom once more grabbed control and righted the Island's crisis by instituting staggered hours. The Jungle Arms was open all night for the workers.

About this time the talkative lady started to bring her dog Upsey along with her. " What a nice little dog," commented Tom. " Next time it comes I'll give it a chloroform biscuit."

Quite as annoying to Tom was the constant criticism of Deryck Guyler's Sir Short Supply, the man always ready to wind red tape round Tommy's projects.

Then there was the night when, instead of saying " Down Upsey " to the yapping dog, Tommy said " Down Monty." There seemed little reason to the radio listeners for this change, but it got a big hand from the studio audience. They knew that Field Marshal Viscount Montgomery was in the studio that night. We had, by the time of this series, moved to the Paris Cinema in Lower Regent Street for our broadcasts, and here we were able to have a fairly large audience. It was very rare that there was not at least one well-known person among our guests. In fact, the competition for tickets became extremely severe, and Francis, Tommy and myself had to exercise diplomacy worthy of a Foreign

Ministers' meeting to avoid giving offence, for only one in a hundred of the people who wanted tickets could get them. We only got four each !

The series ended in June, and within a few weeks Tommy was off to America.

CHAPTER XXI

AMERICA AND AFTER

ON June 24th Tommy went abroad for the first time when, in company with Francis Worsley and me, he boarded the *Aquitania* on his way to New York via Canada. It had been uphill work getting him to leave England ; until the very last moment I thought he would back out and now, looking back on the trip, I doubt if he really enjoyed it. He was so set in his habits, so devoted to his home, so incapable of throwing all care aside in order to relax completely for a few weeks, that although outwardly the " life and soul of the party," inwardly he disliked going and, when there, wished he was at home.

And yet, as I will show, he was an instantaneous success on the air in New York ; he had many offers to stay on, vast fees were offered him : it is possible, indeed, that he would have proved as big a star in the States as he was on our own B.B.C. I do not believe that he was tempted by all those offers or by the prospect of making a fortune ; he just wasn't " at home " in New York, and, although he was delighted to see his name in lights on Broadway, he could not have stood the amount of ballyhoo with which the publicity boys would have surrounded him ; he would have hated the boom and boost, the noise and glitter, the tension and nervous strain which appear to be essential in order to put over a programme in America. He was, he felt, too old, too tired to face it. " Let's go back to England ; this place is too hot, too hectic, too hysterical."

Francis and I had certainly plotted and planned, connived at his going and cajoled him to go. He had spent eight years in ITMA now ; we were all getting a bit stale ; we needed new scenes, new characters, a new set-up ; but our general intention in visiting the States was first of all a holiday and then a kind of re-fresher course studying American radio. No arrange-ments had been made for him to broadcast, and no preliminary publicity had been fixed ; he was already well known there as a radio star—not so much to the American public who couldn't understand ITMA any-way—but to radio people—the Bob Hopes and Jack Bennys and other top-liners who had met him, heard him, and whom he had helped in their visits here. They were amongst his greatest admirers, and so were the radio chiefs of all the big networks in a land where the exploitation of artistes and programmes had become a major industry.

It was, then, a change of scene and sound we were in need of rather than a search for new ideas, and we certainly found it. For three men of vastly varying tastes and habits to travel together, to share cabins and to be constantly in each other's company, is to take a risk that few partnerships have ever survived, but—thanks to Tommy's ever kindly and equitable disposition—we were still talking to each other when we got back after being away from home for just over five weeks.

The *Aquitania* was still in war-time trim. Orders were given over the ship's loud-speaker system. Tommy couldn't be kept away from the mike, and one after-noon passengers heard a voice boom out : " Will the gentleman who picked up a piece of rare old china on the promenade deck kindly meet her at the same place to-night ? "

It was Tommy up to his tricks.

At Halifax, Nova Scotia, we were welcomed with banners on the landing-stage. " Welcome to ITMA ! " " Welcome to That Man Again ! " " Good Old Tommy ! " Carrying the banners were British war brides who still remembered Tommy's broadcasts. They dragged Tommy ashore, and for two hours he chatted to them in the grilling sunshine. When he escaped—speechless with thirst—he found that Halifax was " dry " and that the ship's supplies were sealed up.

Reporters besieged us at Montreal, and later New York. It was not intended that Tommy should broadcast in the U.S.A., but he did—three times. He made such a hit that he got many offers to stay. This success, I believe, was due to two things. American radio programme sponsors recognised in him a great broadcasting comedian, speaking a type of English they could understand, and Tommy was so far removed from their ideas of the " la-di-da " Englishman or the " Limey."

Then came the day when Tommy saw his name in lights on Broadway. " GULF PETROL PRESENTS TOMMY HANDLEY IN ' WE, THE PEOPLE '." Tommy fairly gulped when he saw the sign over the Hammerstein Theatre.

Fêted in New York and Washington, he was taken to the Senate, to Congress and to the headquarters of U.N.O. at Lake Success (where he met so many friends that he almost missed the afternoon session). And how delighted he was when, trying to cool off in the heat of New York, we took the ferry to Staten Island and found a signpost pointing to New Brighton ! " It's just like crossing the Mersey," he said.

At our hotel, Tommy worked one of his most elaborate gags. Among our letters of introduction was one to a gentleman whom we were always going to meet, but never did. Yet, after midnight, my bedside 'phone would ring. There would be our friend (or so I thought) inviting me to week-ends in the Adirondacks, or bathing parties at Long Island. He always had Walter Winchell, Bing Crosby, Jack Benny or Fred Allen with him. He was always able to recall where we had been that evening, and would regret that he had just missed us.

Knowing Tommy as I did, I can't think why I never tumbled to the fact that it was just " That Man " again, pulling my leg ! It was Francis Worsley who first discovered the hoax.

And so back to England in the *Empress of Canada* ; landing at Liverpool with the Lord Mayor waiting to greet his townsman, the ex-Mayor of Foaming-at-the-Mouth. Then on to meet Tommy's mother and his brother Jack and sister-in-law Nance. Despite rationing they had a grand meal ready for us. We enjoyed it better than any we had in America, and washed it down with a bottle of good English beer. (America hasn't got everything !)

During all this time we never discussed ITMA. Francis spent most of his time in New York in Radio City and in discussions with the high-ups on questions of production and technique. I was writing a series of articles for the London *Evening Standard*, and we met at night and wandered far in the cool of the evening. Tommy probably saw more of Manhattan than either of us. He had read a great deal about New York and, strangely enough, in the most modern city in the world, he was always searching for the oldest and most historic spots. His greatest thrill was, I believe, to wander into the Metropolitan Opera House and to sit in Caruso's dressing-room. We stayed at the New Weston Hotel beside St. Patrick's Cathedral, and rarely a day passed that he did not visit it—there was something there that appealed to him, but it was the old haunts he loved to seek out. The newness of New York made no appeal. No matter how successful he might have been on the air in America he would never have felt at home there. How refreshing to him must have been the smell of the Mersey !

Soon after our return we were back on the air with our new series in which Sophie Tuckshop (Hattie Jaques) was born and Frisby Dyke, the Liverpudlian, was introduced.

It was fitting that that series should refer to Tommy's American trip. Our radio licence permitted us, of course, to move his friends to Liverpool, and the generous hospitality of the Captain of the *Empress of Canada* was changed when the microphone eavesdropped on Tommy's farewell to the Captain, to the latter's order : " Get off my ship and never darken my poop again." The Liverpudlian accent of " Hello, Folks ! " had been replaced by a Yankee twang, and words like " swell " had crept in. But Tommy soon realised he was back from the land of great thick steaks to the land of pale fish cakes.

Old friends were still around to comfort him in the awful news from Sir Short Supply that Tommy must report at a Labour Exchange and be directed. There was the Colonel, for instance, who was eager to introduce a friend. This is the dialogue from the first programme of the series :

JACK TRAIN : Allow me to introduce a man I esteem very highly.

TOM : Your keeper ?

JACK : No, sir—my brewer—Willie Watery Wallop.

TOM :	How are you, Watery ? Are you one of the Wallops of Hope Pole Street ? Where did you two meet ?
JACK :	In an antique shop in New York.
TOM :	Antique shop ?
JACK :	Well, sir, it must have been—place was full of bottles of whisky. Wasn't it, Willie ?
DERYCK :	Quite right, Humphrey, quite right.

Tommy duly reported to the Exchange and was appointed to the position of Industrial and Scientific Adviser to His Majesty's Government.

The second show of the series came from Radiolympia, the first radio exhibition since 1939, and played before a packed audience in the special theatre built inside the hall. Tommy's first job in his official capacity was naturally to investigate the radio industry. In a later programme he interested the Government by his new method of industrial psychological selection of staff, and then in October Sir Stafford Cripps was supposed to have sent him a succinct order to present England to the world as the finest country on earth. Tommy's solution of the problem was to organise a pageant.

Early in November we had news that brought us as great a thrill as the letter from Windsor Castle earlier on. As part of the celebrations of the Silver Jubilee of the B.B.C., the Royal Family were to visit Broadcasting House, and ITMA was chosen to represent Radio Variety. The broadcast was to be switched from the Paris Cinema to the Concert Hall of Broadcasting House, and it was to be televised. It was thus two great occasions in one. We decided that, in view of the honour conferred on us by the B.B.C., Tommy should make an inspection tour of Broadcasting House—something which would probably appeal to Their Majesties who had, of course, seen the various studios and offices in the building on previous visits. The script of this show stands out from the serried ranks lying in the long files kept in an annexe to Broadcasting House because it is on light green paper—the colour used to avoid reflection from the lights. It is, of course, almost unique for a television cast to use scrips at all, but this was an ITMA show primarily for sound broadcasting, and there was no desire to make it a television show first and foremost. The Emitron cameras were allowed to peep in, as it were.

The Concert Hall was filled with a specially invited audience, and when the Royal party—the King, the Queen, and Princess Margaret—entered, they were given a tremendous welcome, typical of the affection of that week of celebration which came not so much from subjects to their King and Queen as from a people who wanted to congratulate a charming and much-loved couple on an anniversary. As such it was quite an informal occasion, and the King, pointing to the programme, was heard to mention various characters of whom the Queen and he were particularly fond. The Royal party, with that punctuality for which they are so famous, had arrived in good time, and the red light flashed as soon as the clock hand flicked to 8.30. So far listeners at home had no idea of the surprise in store for them. Then came the announcement which was to give a start of excitement to millions of listeners who almost sub-consciously hear the programme key announcement.

" This is the B.B.C. Home Service," said John Snagge. " Your Majesties, Your Royal Highness, Ladies and Gentlemen, ITMA ! "

The programme opened with some gentle flirting

between Hotchkiss and Sir Short Supply, both teeter-
ing on the edge of matrimony, and their *tête-à-tête*
was interrupted as Tommy descended down the
chimney, rehearsing for Christmas. He explained :
" I'm Sir Stafford Clause, Hotch, and if you're not
a good girl I'll put a photo of Mr. Strachey in your
stocking."

Then he was off on his investigation of Broadcasting
House. On his way he caused delighted laughter from
the Royal guests in his meeting with his talkative lady
friend. " Down, Corgi—I mean Upsey," he said.
Tommy seemed surprised to find the band in evening
dress—" I wonder what the waiters at the Athenæum
are wearing to-night ? " he asked. Rae Jenkins ignored
the remark, but he told Tommy he had a special treat
for him—the song game they used to play at boys' camps
before the war : " Underneath the Spreading Chestnut
Tree," with actions. This was, of course, one of the
famous events at the camps for public school boys and
workers' sons which were always attended by the King
when he was Duke of York, and the subject of an historic
news-reel. So the tour went on : the B.B.C. insurance
man ; Mona Lott bringing Stuart Hubberd's washing ;
the children's studio with the whimsyish notice, " Twans-
mission in pwogwess—watch the wed light " ; the announcers' card-room, and so forth. Tommy soon had
his own programme organised, with girls in bathing-
costumes running the early morning physical jerks.
This was the cue for Hotchkiss to enter. She took one
look and protested :

" It's disgusting. Who's listening to this rubbish,
anyway ? "

" You'd be surprised ! " said Tommy.

After the programme ended the whole ITMA team

was presented to the King and Queen and the Princess. His Majesty told Tommy that he very rarely missed ITMA, and often listened to the repeats as well. " I missed the one on the day of the Wedding," he added. " I'm told it was especially good. But you know how it is with weddings." The Queen said that she was sure " Elizabeth and Philip would be sorry to have missed coming." The young Royal couple did, as a matter of fact, make an informal visit to the Paris Cinema during a later ITMA show after their return from Scotland. It was quite informal, and they stayed on after the show. Princess Elizabeth reminiscing about Tommy's visit to Windsor, and Prince Philip talking about ITMA and the Navy.

Tommy opened 1948 with his fuel-saving campaign, and then in February there were ominous signs of decay in the Colonel's friend, Willie Wallop. The return to second childhood was obvious when Tommy saw him. " Good heavens—look at his trousers held up with a safety-pin, and look at his moustache all covered with syrup of figs. Isn't that so, Willie ? "

" Quite wight, Uncle Tommy, quite wight," Willie replied.

Worse still was the change in his drinking habits. As the Colonel explained : " It's terrible, sir ; he insists on standing outside the public with the other children drinking fizzy lemonade and shouting ' When are we going home ? ' through the door."

At this period Tommy always had an interview with a man who started quietly and ended up with a shout. Here's an example of their routine :

HUGH MORTON : Good morning, I thought you'd like to know I've just caught a beauty.

TOM : Oh, really—where ?

Hugh :   On the Embankment.   What a struggle I had——

Tom :   I bet you did.   Did it take long ?

Hugh :   Oh yes, best part of thirty minutes.   You see, the first two got away.

Tom :   What size was the one that you caught ?

Hugh :   The usual size—about as big as this room.

Tom :   As big as this room !   You never caught a fish the size of this room ?

Hugh :   You misunderstand me.   I never said I caught a fish.   I CAUGHT A TAXI.

There was also Fred Yule's hearty character who thumped Tom on the back to press home every point in his conversation.   It was a relief to Tommy when the conversation closed with a roar : " Wait till I tell the boys," and this full-time bore took himself off.

Fred's other well-known character in this series was Atlas, the man in a delicate state of health.   He looked all right, but explained : " You can't go by appearance. I'm apt to change colour any moment.   Me run a message, Mr. Handley ?   Me ?   In my state of health ? "

The series was, indeed, particularly successful in the creation of new characters, and new angles for the existing ones.   Tommy's own favourite at this time was his word discussions with Frisby Dyke.   Most listeners will recall them.   They went like this :

Tom :   . . . Moving slowly over the cobblestones comes a tumbril with its hideous paraphenalia.

Deryck Guyler : What's paraphenalia ?

Tom :   In the—eh ?

Deryck : I said what's paraphenalia ?

Tom :   You stand there looking like an English chorus boy in " Oklahoma " and say you don't know what paraphenalia means ?

Deryck : Never heard of it.

TOM :   Well, it's the same as kerosenalia—only you
            use paraffin.

DERYCK :   Fancy that !

TOM :   Now listen, Frisby Dyke : aren't you the
            Tooting man who makes bulbs for motor
            horns ?

DERYCK :   No, I'm learning to be a slop.

TOM :   A policeman ? Are you studying crime at
            Scotland Yard, London ?

DERYCK :   No—Scotland Road, Liverpool.

TOM :   Fancy that. Where was I ?

DERYCK :   On the tumbril, Tom.

A close competitor for the favourite sequence was
that of Hattie Jaques' Sophie Tuckshop :

TOM :   Hello, little girl !

HATTIE :   My teacher says I mustn't talk to strange
            men. Hello !

TOM :   Why, it's that sweet-eating schoolgirl. This is
            going to be a bit sticky. How are you, my dear ?

HATTIE :   Very well. Would you like a peppermint ?
            They've come loose in my pocket.

TOM :   Thanks. I'll have the one with the blue
            serge fluff on . . . It's a bit hard, isn't it ?

HATTIE :   Oh, I've made a mistake. That isn't a sweet.
            It's a button off my blouse.

TOM :   Eh ? Are you sure it's off your blouse ?
            How are you getting on at school ?

And so on, amid a welter of food, giggles and re-
gurgitations, always finishing with the phrase " . . . but
I'm all right now."

Nationalisation of almost everything, including jokes,
women for industry, the ITMA tourist board—the
series pointed a derisive finger at the news of the moment,
until in June came the final show of the eleventh series,
and the two hundred and ninety-fourth since 1939.

Miss Hotchkiss brought Tom a telegram in which it was stated : " Report to Home Office at once."

" I know what I've done," said Tommy. " I've been working too hard. My Union's complained."

There was a lot more truth in the first part of this statement than any of us guessed, though we had our suspicions—those of us who knew him best. Tommy was not—though it was virtually impossible to realise it —a young man. The strain of a show which had run on and on was beginning to show. He was often very tired by the week-end when he left for a few hours' recreation at his country cottage. We suggested that he should ease up a little on the charity shows, the interminable letter-writing. Francis even hinted that we might suggest to the B.B.C. that the next series started later than its usual September, but he pretended not to understand. To him the old, old maxim of the veteran player : " The show must go on " wasn't just a cliché.

CHAPTER XXII

THE PENALTY OF FAME

STORIES about Tommy Handley, by the end of the war and just afterwards, became so widespread that many of them, to put it mildly, must be written off as apocryphal. It was a perpetual delight to Tommy to look through the press cuttings which gave stories purporting to be inside dope by gossip writers, and reporters who were on the spot. Many of them were as new to Tommy as they were to the readers.

In point of fact there was little need for these flights of fancy, for truth was invariably funnier than fiction where Tommy was concerned. The anecdotes which follow are at least authentic. They have been picked at random from my memory of a bizarre and joyous decade of ITMA exploits.

The show's catch-phrases were, of course, the trade marks with which Tommy was greeted wherever he went, and there were cases where they caused laughter in which he played no part. In fact, some people must have very reasonably wished they had never been invented. Writers had to be careful not to use parallel phrases, and worse than that was to give a cue which could expect an ITMA answer. No one can blame Shakespeare for taking risks of this sort, but is it a fact that " Macbeth " had to be changed because of an ITMA reference. An actor voiced the Bard's line " What is a traitor ? " in just the tone that Naieve used.

There was a burst of laughter, and next night the line was altered. Tchekov's "Uncle Vanya" got similar treatment when presented at the Westminster Theatre in 1944. In one tremendously dramatic scene, with the audience at concert pitch to know what was happening, a shot rang out off-stage. An actor rushed on, flourishing a still smoking revolver. "Missed him," he shouted, and the dramatic build-up was ruined as gusts of laughter swept the auditorium.

Then there was the provincial try-out of Eric Linklater's play, "Crisis in Heaven," at the Opera House, Manchester. Barry Morse played the part of Pushkin, the Russian poet, and in one of his long and rather pompous speeches he finished with the words : "I go."

Just as if they had been rehearsed for the part, the audience replied with one voice : "I come back."

Several clergymen wrote in to say that they had to watch with an eagle eye for signs of amusement with some lines of the hymns and psalms which were dangerously close to ITMA phrases, but it is significant that none of them ever complained about this. In fact, most of them went out of their way to commend Tommy for his work in helping people with laughter during the troublous times of war. There was even a Brighton parson who announced that the subject of his sermon would be : "What *me*, in *my* state if health ? "

Hundreds of church organisations wrote to Tommy asking him to come along and open a bazaar or just be here, if he could spare a few minutes. To the best of his ability he tried to fit in these charity affairs when time and distance permitted, and by his express wish they were not used for personal publicity. The world at large had no idea that he was visiting some small village, though in the neighbourhood it was probably the great day of the year. He was at his brightest and best with children, and being a boy at heart until the day of his death he genuinely enjoyed any affair where there were large numbers of children, often wrecking some carefully planned programme by staying far longer than the schedule arranged.

To me, some of the most unforgettable sights were at the Children's Hour pantomimes written by Dorothy Worsley during the war. They were performed in an actual theatre, and they went on long after the transmission was over. For days before these performances took place the B.B.C. and Tommy were stormed by hundreds of letters and personal visits from children wanting tickets, and it was Tommy who thought of the fairest solution—draws by ballot at various schools and homes. On the day of the show itself in the street where the theatre stood there would be a solid jam of children ; police had to be called in to keep order. Children waited for two hours while the show was on in order to catch Tommy and the other artistes coming out, and the sight of that sea of waving autograph books was enough to daunt the bravest man.

The autograph business was always a problem for Tommy. To satisfy everyone would have meant wrecking the carefully-planned schedules (impossible, of course, in the case of a broadcast) ; to ignore them would have meant disappointment of the kind that only a child can feel. Often he would have the books collected and would spend every second he could during the show signing his name over and over again so that the book could be handed back later to the kiddies patiently waiting outside. Inevitably there would be some tear stained youngster left whose bit of paper had been los in the general scramble. He got an autographed photograph to make up for it.

One of his happiest occasions with children was the opening of the Children's Corner at the London Zoo in 1945. Most of the ITMA company went along as well, and for a report of this affair I cannot do better than quote, of all papers, the *Lancet* (June 2nd, 1945) :

" The sun shone down on us, the lamb bleated, and the press of children with their next-of-kin inside the gates was only exceeded in density by the solid crust of children wedged enviously against the locked turn-stile.

" Somebody passed Mr. Handley another animal. He had already welcomed a fox-cub ('I've brought this for you, sir,' Mrs. Mopp murmured lovingly), a horrified gosling, and the lamb. At our feet a dingo pup was capably tearing his way through the sacking roof of his box, and Donald Duck, detained in a basket, was giving a gala demonstration of temper.

" We were among the privileged guests at the re-opening of the Children's Zoo—one of the first and best of peace-time pleasures to come back to us ; and there were Mr. Handley, and Mrs. Mopp, and Sam, and So-So, and the Colonel and all the other looking-glass creatures of ITMA, as large as lions and nearly as natural, in our very midst.

" ' Why does he have to be in a box ? ' asked David, watching the tireless dingo. In a sun-suit *décolleté* to the waist and terminating unexpected in long blue linen trousers, David looked his age—rising four. (This was David Drury, Jean Capra's elder son.)

" ' It's a surprise for Mr. Handley,' replied his grandmother, who looked considerably less than hers.

" ' Why does Mr. Handley have to have a surprise ? ' David wanted to know ; and Mr. Handley, who had just been supplied with a parakeet, looked as though he would be glad to know too. The bird was white with a sky-blue tongue, a beak fit to chisel concrete, and prominent cynical eyes lidded and encircled with blue shagreen. He sat on Mr. Handley's shoulder and seemed to be considering whether to take an ear or an eye for luncheon. Fortunately he was vegetarian.

"So was the half-grown kid who came next, and devoured the Handley buttonhole. ('What a showman, eh?' So-So exclaimed admiringly.)

"But at last the animals ran out, and Mr. Handley, having declared the Children's Zoo open ('Did you say they were open, sir?' asked the Colonel), stepped down from his trial a free man, without a stain on his character, and we all went off to see the Mouse Town."

It was, of course, a little surprising to see such a report in the columns of an august medical journey, and Tommy added it to his collection of unusual quotes. Another one was in a Russian magazine published in the Soviet Union during the war to foster relations between the two countries. There was a large photograph of Tommy Handley at the microphone bearing the words underneath :

TOMMN X3HAMEN

The Russians heard of Tommy Handley in other ways, thanks to the bright idea of a British soldier. High up on the Semmering Pass in the mountains separating the British and Soviet Zones of Austria the two road barriers were about a hundred yards apart. Just after V.E.-Day, on a Russian suggestion, the respective guards were marched by their N.C.O.'s to a spot half-way across "No Man's Land," and formal greetings were exchanged. The British wished their friends "Good night," and the Soviet troops reciprocated with that well-known term of adieu " Okay." This sufficed for several weeks, when a Soviet corporal suggested that the whole thing was far too short to be a proper slice of ceremonial. He suggested that arms should be presented in honour of their leaders as well. And so the rifles clicked to the present in honour of Marshal Stalin, then for Winston Churchill, and so on down through various generals. The Russians were able to provide a far longer list than the Cockney corporal who ran out of ideas after naming Montgomery, Alexander and his own corps commander. Getting rapidly fed-up with a ceremonial which looked like taking half the night, he shouted " In honour of Tommy Handley—present hipe." And there, in the gathering darkness of the Austrian mountains a dozen or so British and Soviet soldiers did the comedian the honours. Night after night, until each group was relieved and posted elsewhere, there were shouts at the changing of the guard : " Zdastvuyet Marshal Stalin " and " Long Live Tommy Handley." It all helped towards the gaiety and friendship of the nations.

Of all the thousands of occasions when Tommy was mobbed I can only recall one occasion when there was something which might be called " Nearly an Ugly Scene." It occurred when he was asked to judge a beautiful girl competition during a holidays-at-home week in a town which had better be nameless. He duly judged the lovelies, with the assistance of the local mayor, M.P., and midwife, and announced the result. Within a few minutes he was surrounded by a mob of irate mothers who demanded to know why their own daughters had not carried off the prizes. He took the scene in good part—he could turn most situations into a joke—and shouted : " Ladies, please. Have a bit of pity for a mere man who has had the most difficult job in his career to-day—that of saying which out of all these pretty girls was to be called the winner. Well, I may say that in all my life I have never seen such a collection of lovely young ladies, but now I see their mothers, and I know why. I congratulate all you ladies on your beautiful daughters."

The irate matrons fairly preened themselves. There were smiles all round. Tommy cocked his hat at a jauntier angle. Things were all right again, thanks to him, but he was always a little dubious about beauty contests after that.

Tommy's hat, by the way, was his trade mark. When he was modelled for Madame Tussauds in 1944 he created a bit of a crisis by saying that his effigy must wear a hat. Strangely enough, nobody keeps a hat on his wax head in Madame Tussauds.

CHAPTER XXIII

THE INEVITABLE FAN-MAIL

I HAVE referred several times to Tommy's interest in his fan-mail. A large number of the letters he received were kept by him at home as souvenirs of a particular programme, and the greater proportion of these were from children. He had a very great love of children and a great understanding of their tastes, as was evident in the Christmas pantomimes and children's parties from the B.B.C. in which he appeared, and where he was able to *ad lib.* to his heart's content.

ITMA, of course, was primarily an adult entertainment, but a very large proportion of his correspondence came from children. They ranged from the mis-spelt messages in block capitals on postcards to really beautifully executed drawings carefully painted in water colours, obviously the result of hours of painstaking work and many rejected false starts.

One co-operative effort which he particularly treasured arrived by post in a roll about two feet wide. Inside was a length of canvas with caricatures all over it. There was a letter from a school teacher who explained that fifteen of her children had drawn portraits of their idea of the chief ITMA characters, and each of the kiddies had enclosed a letter. These were some of them :

" DEAR TOMMY,—I hope you are well and I heard you on the wireless and you was good and I painted

some pictures of you the ones that make me laugh are
wlo booger and bigga bangger and the lad that pings
and pongs and tell Miss Hochiss not to scold you love
from FRANK S——."

" DEAR TOMMY,—We listen to you on the radio every
week and you dont half like it I bet. I like fany rot
cake too. I like niev too and we are sending you some
paintings and I hope you laugh at them in doors I think
all the people laugh too. From GILLIAN C——."

" DEAR TOMMY,—We have painted some pictures of
you. We hear you on the radio. I have done Mrs. Mop
and Miss Hotchkiss I hope you like our paintings you
make me laugh tell the chin strap not to drink so much
bear. Love from LESLIE G——."

" DEAR TOMMY,—We are sending you some paintings
we listen to you on the radio every week and on Sundays.
It is nice you make me laugh in bed. I like Miss hotch
Kiss I like you too I like the kernl as well I like bigga
banger you make my Mother laugh too I like your show
I love it. Love VALERIE ANN E——."

To these kiddies there was little make-believe about
the programme. The place, the people, and the adventures were real, and Tommy had to be most careful in
his replies not to destroy that illusion. For instance,
if a child's letter arrived addressed to Governor Handley,
Tomtopia, c/o the B.B.C. London, then he would not
answer it for a week or so in order to allow for the
difficulties of long distance mail. He enquired as to the
possibility of having a special stamp for these children's
letters but it was, of course, not feasible. However, the
address which he made up usually kept up the idea of
a distant land, a farm, Foaming-in-the-Mouth, or wherever the current adventure was. Incidentally, the risks
Tommy ran through Lefty's constant efforts to shoot

him caused a large number of worried letters from children, and it was at least a contributory cause of the final reform of that bizarre character, who, it may be remembered, at last agreed with his pal Sam that the boss was swell and deserved no longer to be used for target practice.

A typical example of the child listener's belief in the reality of Tommy's adventures is shown in the following letter received in June, 1945 : " DEAR MR. HANDLEY,— " Is it true that you are going on holiday ? Because last night you said to Mrs. Mop that you would pay them all their wages next Thursday and she said you would not be there on Thursday. Could you come here during your holiday. I have learnt to row with two oars. We can lend you a pair of Pop's water boots because the dinghey leaks a bit. I will show you my kitten. Love from SHEELAH W."

And as to their belief in Tommy's omnipotence the following request gives a little evidence. " DEAR TOMMY, —ITMA is too late. I go to bed at 7 o'clock. Please put it on early on Sunday. From JEREMY CLERK, aged 6½ years. T.T.F.N."

Also treasured by Tommy were the letters from parents in which they mentioned the love their children, large and small, held for the programme. They were ungrammatical and a little incoherent ; probably the longest letters to strangers the writers had ever tackled in their lives. But they had that touch of spontaneous, genuine affection which Tommy seemed to be able to engender so well over the air. There was, for instance, the letter from a woman in Rotherham, which arrived after Tommy's illness in the spring of 1945 :

" DEAR SIR,—I feel it my duty to thank you from the bottom of my heart for all the lovely evenings we have

shaired with you in your broadcasts we have a little girl
seven years her name is Janet she thinks there isnt anyone else in the whole world like you. She has a picture
of you taken with that little dolly of Mrs. Mop she calls
you her little cave man and when you was ill she was
very upset she'd take your picture out of her little desk
look at you and say to her father and I. I do hope
you get better and when it was broadcast you was better
she clapped her hands and danced round the house
like a little feather you see Sir we would have spent
many lonely hours if it hadnt been for you coming into
our home when Janet's daddy was on the home guard
you always cheered us very much when otherwise we
should very often been reduced to tears and you also
helped us to win this great victory helped our fighting
men and women to keep there spirit up with your lovely
jokes and may God bless you and help you in your
work which has proved so successful to us all please
exuse my very humble letter bye bye until Thursday.
I am, Yours truly, E.M."

Then there were the letters which came from far-away
places, from people who listened to the programme on
the Empire or North American services. One, received
in November, 1942, was from an American living in
Hattiesburg, Missouri, U.S.A. " This is written to let
you know how much your broadcasts are appreciated
by the British boys training here in America. For
several months I have had groups of these boys visit
me while they are on leave from their duties. They
have come here from all parts of the United States and
Canada, and I have really enjoyed having them here.
I think that one of the things that they enjoy most is
the opportunity to get around the short-wave radio and
listen to your programs.

" You may be interested to know that the next thing they most enjoy is a trip to New Orleans to hear some of the negro boogie-woogie players on Bourbon Street. In fact it is sometimes difficult to get them out of those places as the negroes seem to enjoy playing for them very much.

" I recently visited a young British seaman in one of our large hospitals here in America. It was on Wednesday afternoon, and he was alone when I arrived. I had brought a portable short-wave radio with me and we turned it on just in time to hear your broadcast. You would understand my motive for writing you this letter had you been able to hear the laughter from that room.

" The very best of good wishes to you on this fine work that you are doing. Sincerely, EARL M——."

As the liberation of Europe proceeded and postal services were restored, letters poured in from European listeners who had learned English via the B.B.C. language lessons so that they could understand the news bulletins and even grapple with the verbal antics of ITMA.

The German intelligence authorities became aware that there was a considerable amount of illicit listening going on during the times of the ITMA broadcasts, and it is believed that they considered the programme was being used either for propaganda or for code messages to the European underground. There were occasions when people who escaped from Hitler's Europe came to Tommy and asked if a piece of music or a sentence could be included so that their families could know they had made the journey safely. This, after suitable investigation by the security authorities, was done. But with these exceptions the German counter-espionage service must have had a terrific task to sort out anything from the sheets of translated dialogue placed on their experts' desks by the Reich Monitoring Service. Or possibly they had a really fruitful source of red herrings. . . .

However that may be, ITMA'S secret audience between 1939 and 1945 was very large. It was, of course, a risky business, as a Burgomaster in a Dutch town realised when there was a thunderous knocking on the door one Friday night after curfew time, which could mean only one sort of visitor. Hastily switching off the radio the Dutchman opened the door—to see the local Gauleiter standing there.

He strode in and glared at the now silent radio set. " You have been listening to ITMA, nein ? "

The Dutchman thought he must have had the set on too loud and nodded helplessly.

The German beamed with pleasure. " That is good," he said ; " I too listen to him. Heil Hitler." He turned and left the house. Only then did the Dutchman realise that Hitler's famous war commentator, General Dittmar, had been interpreting the war from the German network at the same time as Tommy explained his Foaming-at-the-Mouth night club scheme from London.

Thousands of European listeners who crouched round carefully toned-down sets for their weekly ITMA didn't understand a word of it. There was, for instance, a message brought by a Polish soldier in 1945 after he had visited his family near Warsaw. " They want to thank you," he said to Tommy, " for the way you helped to keep up their morale during all those years. They cannot speak or understand a word of English, of course, and so they did not listen to the English news bulletins. But they liked and understood ITMA because of the laughter. There was no laughter within the borders of Poland in those years." For large numbers of voluntary exiles from the Mother Country ITMA brought a whiff of home, as is shown by the following letter received in June, 1946 :

"Estancia,"

Province of Buenos Aires,

Argentine Republic.

" DEAR TOMMY HANDLEY,

" I feel I must write and tell you how we all enjoy your performances of ITMA which we get over here so clearly from the B.B.C.

" The reception comes over just as if you were in the same room, and I do not miss a word of the fun, you can imagine to a bloke like myself who has not been Home for the last 10 years, 1936 my last trip, your fun is like a whiff of real England.

" The latest about the Health Centre and the Cricket, was great, believe me you keep me glued to the seat in front of the radio, and I wish you could hear our laughs, its great.

" The Colonel, old chin strap, is wonderful, and reminds me of so many of that ilk, we had in the last war, of the Old School Tie type.

" ' Ain't it a shame ' I would like to meet, though I give you Miss Hodgkiss ! What intrigues me so much, is as to how you put on these damned good shows, are you dressed up, in special togs, and what does your scenery consist of, is it on a stage, with an audience ? I am very taken with the door that you people continually go in and out of. Perhaps you might get the B.B.C. to reproduce in their *London Calling*, which I receive, how your show is worked, etc., *and* please some photos of the charming ladies that aid you in your wonderful show.

"We are ranching here, cattle and sheep in hill and sierra country, miles from any town and a night's train journey from Buenos Aires.

"Naturally, it is all Spanish, and so the B.B.C. is tremendously appreciated. I used to enjoy the Co-optimists during last war, the Byng Boys, Leslie Henson, etc., etc. I would give all the cows in Argentina to see a good English show again of those sorts.

"Wishing you the best of luck, and good hunting, and may your ITMA shows never grow less, and remember we are listening to you many thousands of miles away and really enjoying it all, and I wish we had you and the Colonel over here, to have one, as whisky is still plentiful, good quality, and not too expensive in Argentina. Sincerely, G.J.V.H."

CHAPTER XXIV

As everyone knows, Tommy died a comparatively wealthy man, leaving more than most of the members of his happy-go-lucky profession. He was, of course, earning a considerable salary from broadcasting, films, stage appearances, commercial advertising, and gramophone recordings during the last ten or twelve years of his life. Judging from the modest way of life that Jean and he pursued, those who knew him well are surprised that he did not leave more. He must have given considerable sums to charity, to old friends of the profession, and for the furtherance of his pet interest, boys' clubs. This interest increased as time went on, and seldom did a week-end pass that he did not visit one, open one, or appear in aid of one. His activities in this direction inspired the inauguration of the Tommy Handley Memorial Fund organised by the Kemsley Press, the proceeds of which will be devoted to the founding of boys' and girls' Clubs and Camps in his home town, Liverpool.

His own interests were tennis and golf, reading and criminology. In latter years the sports did not interest him so much, and he became a keen cyclist instead, possibly from experience of the advantages of this method of locomotion when we were dispersed at Bristol and Bangor. On the subject of criminology he was an expert, with an encyclopædic knowledge of the best in

both fiction and fact.   He could outline the plots of
the most famous cases of Lord Peter Wimsey, Poirot,
Trent, Paul Temple, and recite the mistakes of such
masters of the art of murder as Crippen, Thorne, Thom-
son and Bywaters, Heath and Seddon.   He often went
to Old Bailey trials at the invitation of friends who
were engaged as Counsel.

In the summer of 1948 Tommy was sitting in court
while the jury retired to consider their verdict in a
murder trial.   The judge's clerk came to Tommy and
invited him into the judge's room to meet Mr. Justice
Birkett.   He stayed chatting for half an hour—an experience of which Tommy was very proud.

Tommy and Jean lived in a flat in Bayswater when
in town.   The London flat was hardly the sort of place
in which to live during the blitz, but Tommy had the
typical tenacity of the North countryman in hanging
on to his home.   In 1941, when they were both in
town on a few days' visit from the B.B.C. activities, a
large bomb fell close to the flat and Tommy was blown
out of bed by the blast.   Jean was unhurt, and although
Tommy was dazed, they both dressed and went down to
see what was going on.   Incendiary bombs had lit up
the Paddington area with a vengeance.   Through the
smoke and soot a local N.F.S. man saw them standing
at the door of their home.

" Come with me, Mr. Handley," he said urgently.
He grasped them both by the arm and hauled them
into the canteen at the fire station, where one engine
crew were having a rest after hours of fire-fighting.

While Tommy stood blinking in the unaccustomed
glare of the lighted room, the fireman turned to him
and said : " You know those gags of yours in ITMA
last Thursday about the plate of porridge.   Well, the

bells went down before we heard the end of them.
Tell us what happened."

While Paddington burned, Tommy gave a repeat
broadcast.

The flat also got on the burglar's list. These enter-
prising gentry do, of course, work out the times when
notable people will be working, and pay an uninvited
visit worked out to schedule. One Thursday in May,
1944, when anyone who cared to find out would know
that Tommy would be rehearsing and a check from the
other side of the road showed that Jean had gone shop-
ping, they duly " effected an entry with a blunt in-
strument."

Jean discovered what had happened. The swag included jewellery, a silver fox fur, some fountain pens,
about £20 in notes—and a ticket for that night's performance of ITMA. The tickets were not, of course,
numbered in any way, and it was impossible to discover
who was using it. Tommy applied his criminological
knowledge as he stood on the stage that night at the
Criterion Theatre assessing the criminal types. There
were several possibles—and one certainty.

During the musical interlude, Tommy managed to
grab a moment and whisper to Francis Worsley : " The
chap in the —— row, —— seat from the right." Francis
had a look through the control room window. " That's
Mr. ——," he said, " a B.B.C. official ! "

A greater nuisance than burglars or bombs was the
telephone jokester. In old telephone directories his name
can still be seen, and during the whole of the war many
thousands of amateur Funfs discovered this fact. Paddington 9905 must have been the busiest number on
the exchange next to the Western Regional station.
Men, women and children rang up to warn " Funf is

on your track ! " to offer " to do you now, sir," and
merely to shout " sompin' terrible's happened." Later
they called to say " Ain't it a shame ? " or " Lovely
grub." If Tommy was unwise enough to ask " Who's
speaking ? " the inevitable reply was " I'll have to ask
me Dad."

The trouble about these calls was that the bright
idea came to people who were celebrating far into the
night. Doubtless the shout of " Good morning—nice
day ! " caused roars of approval at some all-night party,
but to Tommy, pulled out of bed at 3 a.m. it was not
so amusing. The calls were a rough barometer of the
success of a programme. A successful one would bring
fifty or sixty calls the same night, particularly after the
Sunday repeat broadcast.

Jean and Tommy tried to solve the difficulty by
saying that the caller had been connected to Paddington Fire Station and ring off. That night brought a
complaint from the Paddington supervisor who was
getting swamped with complaints of defective lines.
Then they tried leaving the receiver off, but the exchange
told them that this wasn't allowed.

The trouble was that amid all these practical jokes
personal or perfectly serious calls would need to be
answered. They could never risk refusing to rise to the
bait. Once Tommy had a good lesson on this subject.
After a programme which featured plenty of dialogue
about the Mer, the exchange rang through to ask
Tommy to stand by for a trunk call. The speaker
said he was the Mer of a Northern town. Tommy
laughed shortly and hung up. The 'phone rang again
and the Mer indignantly complained at the way Tommy
had hung up on him. He really was a Mayor and
wanted Tommy to help in a charity show.

At last, in 1946, the Post Office came to the rescue with a private number.

One other place in London which saw a lot of Tommy was the Savage Club. He spent many hours there, and used a lot of the time writing letters. How many letters he wrote a week no one will ever know. His immense mail from all parts of the world reached him via the B.B.C. and direct from the Post Office when addressed "Tommy Handley, London," "The Governor, Tomtopia," and even "ITMA." He read all these letters. There were piles of them around his flat and country cottage. They were in his pockets and at his club. Not many people thought enough to enclose a stamped envelope, but they got a reply just the same. Nor was it a stereotyped reply, unless the B.B.C. had so many that it was simply essential to get up to date. This was exceptional, however, and usually the letter was addressed individually with some reference to the remarks made by the writer. Undoubtedly Tommy, great human person as he was, did not realise what these personal notes meant to the recipients. I confess I did not until the *Radio Times* inserted a request for memories of Tommy for the purpose of this biography. Then those letters started rolling in. Some were still immaculate and bore the traces of adhesive where they had been in an album ; others were crumpled and yellowed with address such as " . . . M.E.F." or " . . . B.A.O.R. Germany." The envelopes in Tommy's writing had been kept as well. They came to me by registered post, with a request that they be returned safely. They came from as far away as Persia, from children who had grown up, from old folks, from mothers who had not forgotten the man who made some kiddie happy with a " get well soon " at the bottom of his brief note.

They came from artists who remembered him, and who were remembered, from the amateur dramatic days, from war-time pals in the R.N.A.S., from Londoners who drove him in taxis.

Individually they contained little news that could be used as an informative item for this book. Some of the letters which accompanied them were quaint and a little incoherent. But in their mass they were a wonderful testimony to the regard with which Tommy held everyone who wrote to him. In their way they were more remarkable than the letters quoted elsewhere which came during Tommy's life.

If Tommy had lived he would have taken a house in Sussex, near Brighton. He grew very fond of that county and that town. Many a time he escaped from London, took the train to Lewes, and from there a bus to Rodmell, where he stayed with Reginald Pound and his wife, who had been close friends of Tommy and Jean for twenty years. The country people of the district had a number of special visits from Tommy. He opened the local flower show and a fête in aid of the local Boys' County Grammar School memorial chapel. In March, 1947, the entire ITMA company gave a show at Wadhurst, just across the border in Kent for a local ex-servicemen's fund in which the dialogue was, as usual in these special shows, given plenty of local colour. In September of the same year he arranged another ITMA show at Heathfield as part of the Battle of Britain celebrations for the village which was known as the graveyard of the *Luftwaffe* due to the number of successful dog fights which took place above the area in 1940.

This glimpse into Tommy's private life may have given the impression that off-stage he was an entirely different person from the man the public knew. If so, this is incorrect. He was, indeed, a man of very simple tastes and liked nothing better than a quiet drink with friends, unrecognised by other folk, but the boy who played pranks in the Liverpool suburbs and the man who clowned on variety stage and in radio studios never really changed. His practical jokes were never-ending, and everyone who had contact with him had to beware of being caught out.

Spoof letters were a favourite form of gag. A typical one was laid on Francis Worsley's desk one day after going through various departments of the B.B.C. and noted for action, and so on. It came from a man living at 10, the Pentygles, Bangor, and indignantly, complained that the producer had failed to turn up for an audition, thus keeping many high-paid artistes waiting to no avail, etc., etc. Closer study revealed that the rather indecipherable signature was that of Parry Goric, the Singing Chemist.

Only very rarely did Tommy's humour cause the slightest embarrassment to the victim. A possible exception occurred in Madame Tussauds, where Tommy found that a know-all had managed to collect for himself an unofficial party of tourists in the Chamber of Horrors. Tommy joined the group.

" Ladies and gentlemen," said the guide and friend, " here we come to the effigy of the most dastardly criminal of the age, Hawley Harvey Crippen, who murdered Belle Elmore. He was the first criminal to be caught by wireless. He was on board the *Majestic* when . . ."

Tommy meekly interrupted to air his knowledge of this crime by pointing out that the name of the ship was the *Montrose*.

The man glared, corrected himself, and finished his story. Then he moved on to the next figure.

"Here we have Mrs. Ogg, who murdered a woman in Highgate and put her body in a pram and pushed it over the Heath. Right here is the very pram she used."

"But surely that pram was burnt in the fire after the first world war?" Tommy protested.

This was too much for the guide. He came over and whispered: "Turn it up, chum. 'Oo are you, anyway?"

It was, of course, very rare for people to have any doubts of his identity. In trains and buses few people would ask him outright. They would start saying phrases from ITMA to one another, while giving sidelong glances at Tommy to see the effect. He had either to acknowledge that he had been discovered or try to bluff it out. The first drew a crowd at the next stop; the latter rarely worked. The result was the same.

CHAPTER XXV

THE LAST ITMA

THE series which was destined never to be completed began on October 13th, 1948—rather later than usual. I have already quoted the opinion of a friend of Tommy's that he dreaded his return to the microphone, and although it was not recognisable on the air—thus making his sudden end all the more surprising—it was apparent to me that he was slowing down. His walk had lost its springiness, he had grown old quickly. When he came to our " sit-rounds " he was a tired man, inclined to doze. Jean was ill, seriously ill—at one time her recovery seemed impossible—and this worried Tommy intensely. He visited her twice every day, spoke constantly of her to Francis and me : it was obvious that he could not face the future without her. Her gradual improvement and her return home revived him considerably, but it was too late—anxiety, the years of effort and constant worry, took their toll. Nothing or no one could convince him that he had many years of broadcasting before him. He must have felt in his bones that this was his last series.

The sixth edition was the three hundredth ITMA, and we were honoured by a visit from Princess Margaret, who came with a party of friends. Diana Morrison presented her with a bouquet from the ITMA cast. But as it was an informal visit no mention was made in the broadcast announcement of the honour the anniversary show had been accorded.

There was a special welcome from all the cast (which now included the Kerbside Choristers, directed by George Mitchell) in the special lyrics for the play-in tune :

> " Sing Happy Days and Auld Lang Syne,
>   He's been that man since one-nine-three-nine.
>   May Mrs. Handley's son
>   In the years to come
>   His gaiety retain.
>   At ninety-three may he still be
>   That man—that man again ! "

Mr. " Itma " was now a resident in Henery Hall, the Tramps' Guest House under the thumb of Matron Hotchkiss. He had been found half a dozen jobs and failed at all of them. His last chance to make good came with a post as night watchman in the waxworks. The Colonel was lurking in the Chamber of Horrors, Atlas was deputising for Henry VIII while the latter went downstairs for a trim-up, Mona was having a cheerful trip through the Chamber, and Sophie was checking up on the taste of waxcakes. They all found a door marked " The Hall of ITMA'S Past." They took listeners on a nostalgic trip back to 1939, and for this reason there were six guest artistes in the programme —the stalwarts who had launched the show in the early days of the war : Dorothy Summers, Horace Percival, Sydney Keith, Clarence Wright, Dino Galvani, and Lind Joyce. It was, therefore the biggest ITMA ever broadcast.

One after the other they came on the air : Funf ; Ali Oop still peddling postcards ; Clarence Wright wishing " Good morning, nice day " and now selling all sorts of things for export only ; Signor So-So exuding joy because he " was happy as a sandbag—it was the

greatest movement of his life " ; Sam Fairfechan honest
to the end with " I have come from my village in Wales
and we all tell each other you're wonderful, but then
you can't believe a word we say " ; Sam Scram giving
it as his opinion that " the celebration of a centenary
signified the stupendous ceremonial splendiferousness of
semi-sesquipedalian sensationalism " ; Bigga Banga talking unadulterated Utopi ; Banjeleo translating it as
" when you come back to Tomtopia Big Chief Income
Tax man wait for you " ; and Mrs. Mopp with a special
birthday cake made out of her own head.

It was a great occasion for Tommy—for all of us.
I believed the listeners loved it too. And less than
three months later we were all to find a little comfort
that we had been able to make this gesture to the well-
loved boss of ITMA. It was hail and farewell.

There were to be ten more shows to the final curtain
on ITMA. On January 5th came No. 310, in which
Hotchkiss had arranged for Tom to become manager
of a tea and coffee stall, Uncle Tom's Cabin. All his
friends called round, of course, and most of them the
familiar ones of the previous year. Worthy of mention,
however, is Basil Backwards, who greeted Tommy with
" Sir—morning good ! Coffee of cup. Strong too not.
Milk have rather I'd." And naturally there was a
visit from Sophie Tuckshop, who invited Tom to come
to a midnight feast if he could bring " sardines and
condensed milk and cream buns and pilchards and
ginger beer and cocoa and doughnuts and sausages."
The Colonel, free from the ghastly Creep, returned
from two weeks of hooch hiking. Frisby had an interesting discussion on the pronunciation of task while
waiting for his date with Penelope (she was in a play
by a whacker called Charles Dickens, writer of two

recent films). Atlas got cross about Tommy laughing
at his tummy (" What's behind it all ? " he protested).
Pogworthy Proudfoot (Poggles) wondered if Tommy
" would frightfully mind if he did a bit of recruiting—
Army, you know " ; the cheeky young Woodley (another
Jack Train character) explained his latest racket of
filling a medicine bottle with coloured water, breaking
it on the pavement and bawling until passers-by contributed a bob or so for replacement. Mona Lott failed
utterly to get cheerful about her election as Miss Water-
works of 1949, and Deryck Guyler's constable got his
l's too prominent in his suggestion of Felonious Intent.

In fact, it was just an ordinary ITMA saga of crazi-
ness. The programme had been used to register Tommy's
new job as café keeper, which seemed to be an ideal
place for him to survey and comment on the passing
scene for many weeks to come. It was not to be. Even
before the recorded transmission had been broadcast
Tommy Handley was dead.

His death, as I have already said, was due to cerebral
hæmorrhage brought on by high blood pressure. He
had awakened with a headache, was dressing to go
out, bent down and collapsed. Jean, herself, just out of
hospital, was alone with him in the flat. She did everything possible for him in his semi-conscious state and
immediately summoned his doctor. He was taken to
a private Nursing Home, a lumbar puncture was performed, but he died within a few hours. Had he lived
he would have been hopelessly paralysed—a terrible fate
for one who had always been so physically and mentally
active. And so this man of many parts, this " King
Jester," this beloved clown, left us. While his voice
was on the air in the 5.30 ITMA repeat, That Man
himself had gone to his reward.

Earlier in the afternoon Francis Worsley had 'phoned me that Tommy had had a stroke, and that there was little likelihood of his appearing that week, and it was when I 'phoned his flat to see how he was that his doctor told me he had gone. I was thus the first of his associates to hear the news. I told Francis, the B.B.C. was informed and on the six o'clock news an incredulous public of many millions was told that : " The B.B.C. regretted to announce the death of Mr. Thomas Handley, the Comedian ! "

To the national and international repercussions to this announcement I have already referred, but typical of many are the following extracts from Dutch papers— one of which, *Vrÿ Nederland*, devoted a whole supplement to an obituary.

A friend in Holland has sent me this translation, which I include exactly as written :

" ITMA KLONK VOORHET LAATST.

ITMA sounded for the last time.

> " Tommy Handley knew how to hold the attention of millions with his weekly radio show for ten years.
>
> " On Sunday evening 9 Januari at 6 o'clock Dutch time, a small boy in London's St. Mary's hospital* tuned in to ITMA. In the room next to him, Mr. Handley lay *opgebaard* (untranslatable).
>
> " Who was he ? History . . .
>
> " Eleven millions in England and uncounted in the Dominions, but also in West-Europe listened every Thursday evening to ITMA. Especially for the English ITMA and T.H. had become a part of their lives and his death means a heavy blow for them. That sounds very exaggerated for Netherlands ears and perhaps unbelievable.

* Actually he died in a private nursing home.

The Dutchman has his favourite actors and variety-artists, but he can nearly imagine that the death of one of them strikes him like a personal loss. But this is the truth. T.H. had something that fetched the people, people of all ages and ranks.

"One should not think that ITMA was cheap of character and therefore easy to follow, on the contrary. To be able to follow the quick pun one had to know well all sorts of idiomatic expressions and of the politics, even where they bore a spoken or local character. . . .

". . . These fixed expressions Handley attached to actual happenings, and he did this so clever and surprisingly, that his show was a coupling of thundering nonsense week after week. Handley's inborn feeling for the caricature for the foolish, that inspires the public and ' does something ' to them. Furthermore his never tiring zeal and punctuality with which the programmes were prepared and Tommy's perfect professional knowledge as a radio artist. The B.B.C. called him the Microphone's best friend.

" To the life of this hard-working man, modest, with the fixed (set) diplomatic face, who received the applause always while standing behind his artists has now abruptly come to an end. It would be impossible to carry on without him.

" Tommy Handley was ITMA."

And again, from the *Luisteraars Logboek :*

" LISTENERS LOGBOOK.

" During a visit to the Netherlands, Sir William Haley, Director-General of the B.B.C. said : ' We can never allow ourselves to have the Handley transmissions start too late. Then the English people would rebel.'

" ITMA started in the heat of the war to let the English, in all grimness, laugh with all their heart.

" Handley always played the man who was the head of a most crazy society, for instance the fantastic Tomtopia. There he had to put order in the business and he had so many fools assembled around him, who cared for so many noisy effects, that he could fire the one wisecrack after the other.

" The power of ITMA was, that there were no limits put to Kavanagh's fantasy. Explosions, inundations, ghosts, voices from the naught, bizarre music—all could be included. Handley always full of beans and very vital of voice, delivered actual commentaries on it, the schooling of a real, city boy betraying.

" Sir Stafford Cripps, the integer and ascetic fighter for British soberness knows a lot of that too.

" ITMA was the pet-show of the English Royal Court. They visited an ITMA repetition not long ago and had themselves televisionised.

" Its That Man Again is now past. There's that voice again the English sometimes will be able to say when the B.B.C. brings up memories from the archives of a fabulous radio success."

And finally, a French paper referring to Tommy, quoted the words that an eloquent member of the Académie Française spoke at the grave of Labiche :

" This good man let us enjoy laughter, loud, sounding, free, large honest, childlike and strong ; the laugh that is not a grin, no dissoluteness, no blasphemy ; the laugh that illuminated our glory, relieved our sorrows and revived our courage."